Special Praise for *All Bets Are Off*

"... *All Bets Are Off* offers an honest, open, frank—
and at times *opinionated*—personal reflection on the
devastation and deception of the disease as it manifests
in gamblers and as it impacts those who love them.

"As a friend of Arnie's and a career Employee Assistance
Professional, I relished the role that Jerry—his new boss at
Jonathan Logan Dresses—played in 1968 when he confronted
Arnie about his gambling, pointed him in the direction of a
twelve-step program, and ultimately set the wheels in motion
for Arnie's walk into the sunshine of recovery and his life of
the past forty-six years free of the stranglehold of his gambling
addiction—all the while with his beloved Sheila at his side.
My hope is that *All Bets Are Off* may be the catalyst
and way forward for many similar journeys."

Bernard E. Beidel, M.Ed., CEAP
Director, Office of Employee Assistance
US House of Representatives

"*All Bets Are Off* exposes the raw reality of friends, relatives,
colleagues, associates, fellow classmates, and just ordinary
neighbors who get caught in the trap of addiction ... gambling
addiction. Denial, deception, depression, and delivery from
thoughts of suicide stare you in the face when you read Arnie's
story. This is not for the weak of heart. It is real."

Stan Morrison
Former Director of Intercollegiate Athletics
University of California, Riverside 1999–2011

"Steve Jacobson is what's known in baseball and journalism as a seasoned pro, a man of credibility, conscience, and caring. Arnie Wexler? There's a reason why, for the last thirty-five years, he has been the news media's go-to guy on issues of addicted gambling: He has saved at least as many souls, including his own, as Mother Teresa."

Phil Mushnick
Sports Columnist, NY Post

"Arnie and Sheila Wexler had the courage to share their story to bring awareness of how problem gambling affects families. Decades have passed, but their story still rings true with many of the same familiar themes in the present-day lives of those afflicted by gambling. We learn and understand the effects of gambling and from this we can bring awareness and prevention; but most of all it gives a sense of hope that we can help, make positive strides, and be nonjudgmental."

Judge Cheryl Moss
Las Vegas, Nevada

"I have known Arnie Wexler for over twenty years. He is a kind and giving man whose story touches a nerve for anyone with an addictive personality. We all know someone who has reached his or her limit; Arnie fought his way back and lived to tell about what it takes to recover and reclaim your life."

Ian Eagle
CBS Sports/YES Network/Westwood One Radio

"Here, at last, is a testament that gives life to the idea that gambling is not a *true addiction*. Largely state-sanctioned gambling allows us to engage in high-risk behavior that we have come to see as an acceptable activity. It continues to grow. It has become an American industry to the point that we now believe in 'family gambling' as a good thing.

"In this intensely personal story, Sheila and Arnie bring home the reality of the dangers inherent in gambling when it becomes an addiction. Gambling, by any and all measures, qualifies as a real medical problem. The more we encourage it the more addicts there will be. More importantly, Sheila and Arnie clearly offer a way out of the hopelessness that strikes at the heart of all addicts. *Read this book.* See if there is anyone you know and can lead on the way to recovery. This is an important treatise that finally brings this hidden problem to the public's eye."

Allan Lans, DO, FASAM
Assistant Professor in Psychiatry,
Columbia College of Physicians and Surgeons
Director of the New York Mets Employee
Assistance Program from 1985–2002

"Just because something is legal, it is not necessarily good or safe. Alcohol is legal, and the misuse of alcohol is responsible for much human misery and humongous losses both in life and money. This is equally true of gambling. Many people are vulnerable to compulsive, addictive gambling, which has resulted in incalculable misery. The compulsion to gamble is one of the strongest drives, ruining families and leading to criminal acts to support the gambling habit. Gambling is not only tolerated socially, but is actually promoted politically. Children are very vulnerable to becoming addictive gamblers, and our culture is paving the way for them.

"No one knows the ins and outs of compulsive gambling better than Arnie Wexler, who has helped literally thousands of people to break loose from this deadly addiction. Arnie has now shared his considerable experience in his book, *All Bets Are Off*.

"This book is a must reading for everyone. The epidemic of compulsive gambling feeds on ignorance. The more we know about compulsive gambling, the more we can protect ourselves and our loved ones from this malignant condition."

Abraham J. Twerski, MD
Medical Director Emeritus and Founder,
Gateway Rehabilitation Center

"I first met Arnie in Nevada in 2006 at a presentation I gave about sports books; he was my validation of my training! I was then fortunate to be a student of both Arnie and Sheila at another conference. I have the deepest respect and admiration for both of them, not only for the help they provide to people, but for allowing me to be both instructor and student."

Deneen L. Hernandez
FBI Forensic Examiner

ALL BETS ARE OFF

ALL BETS ARE OFF

LOSERS, LIARS, AND RECOVERY FROM GAMBLING ADDICTION

✕ ✕ ✕ ✕ ✕ ✕ ✕ ✕ ✕ ✕ ✕ ✕ ✕

ARNIE AND SHEILA WEXLER
WITH STEVE JACOBSON

CRP®
CENTRAL RECOVERY PRESS

LAS VEGAS

Central Recovery Press (CRP) is committed to publishing exceptional materials addressing addiction treatment, recovery, and behavioral healthcare topics, including original and quality books, audio/visual communications, and web-based new media. Through a diverse selection of titles, we seek to contribute a broad range of unique resources for professionals, recovering individuals and their families, and the general public.

For more information, visit www.centralrecoverypress.com.

Publisher: Central Recovery Press
3321 N. Buffalo Drive
Las Vegas, NV 89129

19 18 17 16 15 14   1 2 3 4 5

ISBN: 978-1-937612-75-7 (paper)
       978-1-937612-76-4 (e-book)

Photo of Arnie and Sheila Wexler by Ivy Wexler. Used with permission.
Photo of Steve Jacobson by Anita Jacobson. Used with permission.

Gamblers Anonymous Twelve Steps printed with permission of Gamblers Anonymous International Service Office.

The Twelve Steps of Gam-Anon have been reprinted and adapted from the original Twelve Steps of Alcoholics Anonymous with approval of Alcoholics Anonymous World Services, Inc. The Gam-Anon Twelve Steps are approved by the Gam-Anon International Service Office, Inc. Permission of the International Service office (ISO) to reproduce the Steps in this volume does not imply affiliation with the writer or publisher. Gam-Anon has no opinion on any of the contents of this volume. Items in italics have been inserted by the writer and are not part of the Gam-Anon Steps.

The Twelve Steps of Gamblers Anonymous and Gam-Anon, are adapted with permission of Alcoholics Anonymous World Services, Inc. ("AAWS"), and are reprinted with permission of Gamblers Anonymous and Gam-Anon. Permission to reprint Gamblers Anonymous and Gam-Anon Steps does not mean that AAWS has reviewed or approved the contents of this publication, or that AAWS necessarily agrees with the views expressed therein. Alcoholics Anonymous is a program of recovery from alcoholism only - use or permissible adaptation of A.A.'s Twelve Steps in connection with programs and activities which are patterned after A.A., but which address other problems, or in any other non-A.A. context, does not imply otherwise.

Publisher's Note: This book contains general information about addiction, addiction recovery, and related matters. The information is not medical advice, and should not be treated as such. Central Recovery Press makes no representations or warranties in relation to the information in this book. If you have any specific questions about any medical matter discussed in this book, you should consult your doctor or other professional healthcare provider. This book is not an alternative to medical advice from your doctor or other professional healthcare provider.

Our books represent the experiences and opinions of their authors only. Every effort has been made to ensure that events, institutions, and statistics presented in our books as facts are accurate and up-to-date. To protect their privacy, the names of some of the people, places, and institutions in this book have been changed.

Cover design by David Hardy
Interior design and layout by Sara Streifel, Think Creative Design

Dedicated to all who suffer from
addiction to gambling
and their family members who suffer with them.
May you find the healing and hope of recovery.

ARNIE AND SHEILA WEXLER

To Anita, for her patience; to Mat, Susan,
Neila, and Greg for urging me to write;
to Delaney, Liam, and Foster—the next generation.

To Arnie and Sheila, for great insight—and to
Sheila for fixing Arnie's spelling.

STEVE JACOBSON

TABLE OF CONTENTS

FOREWORD ix
Rob Hunter, PhD, Founder, Nevada Psychological
Associates and Problem Gambling Center of Las Vegas

ACKNOWLEDGMENTS. xv

INTRODUCTION xvii

PROLOGUE. xxvii

1 WHEELING AND DEALING 1

2 CRAFT AND GRAFT 17

3 BOTTOMLESS QUICKSAND 31

4 PAY FOR PLAY 47

5 ON THE BRINK 65

6 TEMPTATIONS AND TIP-OFFS TO TROUBLE 77

7 TWELVE-STEP RECOVERY FOR COMPULSIVE 97
GAMBLERS AND THEIR FAMILIES

8 NEW LIFE 127

9 THE BIG PICTURE. 143

ADDITIONAL RESOURCES 159

A WORD FROM STEVE JACOBSON. 165

FOREWORD

THE TERM "LIVING LEGEND" is certainly overused, but still remains a valid descriptor for the rare and special individual.

While those endowed with this title are usually popular celebrities—artists, athletes, and entertainers (and the occasional chef or skateboarder)—I believe that, in fact, living legends do exist, and sometimes in other, more important fields.

Arnie Wexler is a living legend.

He has spent all forty-six years of his recovery from gambling addiction embodying one of the most important tenets of twelve-step recovery, the Twelfth Step itself—reaching out to those who still suffer.

The countless thousands of lives Arnie has touched is unmatched in twelve-step service work.

Arnie's work with addicted athletes and the sanctioning bodies that regulate athletics, such as the NBA, NFL, and NCAA, is similarly extraordinary.

His proactive involvement with the growing gaming industry is also without equal. Serving as an advocate for those in need of assistance and understanding, Arnie has presented his knowledge of both the complex physiology underlying gambling addiction and recovery from the disease to executives at the helm of many of the country's leading casinos.

His good wife Sheila, whose experiences during Arnie's gambling years represent family members impacted by the devastation of compulsive gambling, has joined him in his outreach efforts. As a couple they have worked with addicts and their families and trained over 40,000 casino workers on gambling addiction and its far-reaching consequences. As a result, they bring support and awareness to all whose lives have been affected.

With an emphasis on family health, gaming industry education, the training tapes they have produced, and the seminars they have led internationally, Arnie and Sheila have set the standard for full recovery from the consequences of gambling addiction.

In the many years Arnie and I have worked together professionally to treat gambling addicts and their families, he has endeared himself to me on several levels. I have lasting memories of both the difficult work he and I have done together and the tremendously fun times we have shared in the process.

We met in 1986 through a significant mutual acquaintance—the late Robert L. Custer, MD, considered the "grandfather" of modern understanding of gambling addiction because his research convinced the American Psychiatric Association in 1980 to include it in their *Diagnostic and Statistical Manual of Mental Disorders.*

Custer was my mentor at Charter Hospital, where I was clinical director for the gambling program, while Arnie was the doctor's friend and an unofficial twelve-step fellowship consultant to us. For reasons of both professional interests and genuine personal rapport, we've since built an everlasting friendship.

As a result, there are many facets of Arnie that I know.

There is the nurturing and emotionally available Arnie who will always help a stranger in need. *Always.*

There is the deeply sensitive and vulnerable Arnie who will share not just the strength and joy of his recovery, but the despair and agony of his active addiction to help others.

And there is still a bit of the "Jersey wise guy" Arnie as well. This persona, I think, has served him well in his absolute refusal to back down from any challenge put between him and the help he brings to other gambling addicts and their families.

Arnie is always available, responding not just emotionally, but physically, to gamblers still suffering. He is a good and loving man, but he is also a tough guy. He's a guy tough enough to have survived the gambling story you are about to read and tough enough to make twelve-step calls that have involved canceling family plans, driving through blizzards, and facing the underbelly of gambling straight on. Arnie is tireless in his efforts to help others.

He is alive with his desire to share the joyous freedom that his recovery has brought him, while still remembering well the horror of his late-stage gambling. When Arnie sees a new person walk into a twelve-step program for the first time, he remembers how he felt that first day he came for help.

You are about to read the story of a legendary recovering addict.

In the following chapters, Arnie explores the hope inherent in the recovery process after smothering in the hopelessness of worsening, ultimately ruinous, fallout from addiction to gambling.

As professionals working within the recovery environment, Arnie and I know that whether rooted in substance abuse or a destructive behavioral practice, addiction is a cumulative and irreversible process. Like any other addiction, gambling addiction is a genuine physiological disease that can only be arrested, not cured. Yet, as Arnie explains so clearly in this book, arresting the addiction is not the end of the process—it is the beginning of a full and meaningful life.

Arnie and Sheila also describe the development of the addiction process, sharing their own history, which started in their youth, developed during early adulthood, and carried destructively into their home and family life. The victimizing effects of gambling addiction on spouses and children are topics known all too well to Arnie and Sheila, and Sheila lends her voice to this topic from her own experience and perspective.

The signs and symptoms of out-of-control gambling behavior that comprise addiction are also included here. As examples, Arnie shares stories of compulsive gambling within the world of professional sports that has dismantled the lives of numerous athletes.

Among the most important components of this book, he provides guidance for entering recovery and describes how to seek it, what to expect within it, and what the addict can look forward to as a result of it. Sheila shares, in her own way, the healing benefits of the recovery process for families. Addiction is commonly defined as a family illness, and that means the family can recover as well, even if an addict does not.

I am proud that Arnie has produced this fine work with the help of Central Recovery Press, who chose to speak out about gambling addiction through his voice of experience.

Like Arnie, the folks at Central Recovery, starting with its selfless founder Stuart Smith, embody the concept of going to great lengths, going that extra mile, to reach out and help others. Assisting those in need is the mission and the strength of Central Recovery, and I am as proud to be a member of that team as I am to call Arnie Wexler my dear friend.

Let's move on now, to "The Legend" speaking on the agony of gambling addiction and the joy of recovery from an addiction as real as any other.

—Rob Hunter, PhD

Consulting Psychologist, Las Vegas Recovery Center

Founder, Nevada Psychological Associates and Problem Gambling Center of Las Vegas

ACKNOWLEDGMENTS

WE ARE GRATEFUL FOR all the support and help of so many who made this book a reality. A special thanks goes out to our many family members and friends. To those who struggle with compulsive gambling and those who love them, we want to say, "Don't give up; there is hope." That is why we wrote this book—to help those who still suffer.

Special thanks go to our children and grandchildren for their support and encouragement, and their understanding of our time spent away devoted to helping others; Jerry Meltzer, Berine Waulkan, Monsignor Joseph Dunne, Frank F, Joe G, Bill B, Carl M, Marty T, Chuck Hardwick, Dan Heneghan, Doc Rena Nora, Carl Zietz, Rob Hunter, Rabbi Abe Twerski, Steve Perskie, Judge Tony Parrillo, Riley Regan, Phil Mushnick, Doc Ira Monka, Doc Mark Blum, twelve-step recovery groups and all the people in recovery,

Florence L, Skip Matti, and Central Recovery Press, especially Patrick Hughes, their sales manager, and Daniel Kaelin, our editor.

Thanks also to the late Robert L. Custer, MD, for his work that resulted in compulsive gambling becoming classified in the medical field as a recognized addictive disorder. He established the first inpatient program for the treatment of compulsive gambling in 1970 at a Veterans Administration hospital in Ohio. He helped organize a compulsive gambling treatment program at Johns Hopkins University. His 1985 book, *When Luck Runs Out,* written with Harry Milt, still rings true. Bob Custer was our friend and he is greatly responsible for our recovery and our dedication to helping people with this affliction.

Finally, we wish to acknowledge and thank all those who walked the path of recovery before us, for their guidance, love, and encouragement.

INTRODUCTION

THIS BOOK HAS BEEN three decades in the making. I've wanted to write this story of the complete devastation of compulsive gambling, and the complete transformation through recovery from it, for everyone affected by this disease. Come to think of it, compulsive gambling wasn't even classified as a medically recognized addictive disorder until several years after I first began thinking about this book.

I've been encouraged in this effort over the years by several other writers, as well as literary agents and publishers. But the timing was never quite right, it seemed, and neither were the resources I needed. I think that's how it is with most things, including the acceptance that a gambling habit has gone from exhilarating to demoralizing and that it finally has to end—you're just not ready 'til you're ready.

But I'm ready now, with the help of my writing partner, Steve Jacobson, whom I've known for years, and the support of my publisher, Central Recovery Press, which understands the stigma of addiction and wants to carry the recovery message of hope to others.

Most people look at gamblers as bad people or crooks, and not as addicted people in need of help.

The message I want to get across is that people who are addicted to gambling, and their families who suffer because of it, can recover and have a good life. Not in my wildest dreams did I ever think our life—my wife Sheila's and mine—could be like it is today. Maybe we can change what the public understands about gambling addiction through our story.

Most people look at gamblers as bad people or crooks, and not as addicted people in need of help. I want to change that perception, and I believe this book will help do that.

Let's start with a story—a heart-wrenching story, like so many stories I hear every day from people in trouble with gambling:

Mom and Dad sit down to study the debts being rung up in their name. They're trying to confront the fact that their son has reached the limits of his credit card. He's been borrowing from his brother and sister. The school says he hasn't been paying his tuition. And aren't some pieces missing from the jewelry box?

Their counselor tells them their son is a compulsive gambler. The parents sigh with relief. Thank God he's only a gambler; at least it isn't drugs or alcohol. They say, "We can be thankful for that."

What a tragic misjudgment these parents have made. Actually, their son's problem may be much worse than alcohol or other drugs. Unknown to most of America, gambling addiction is a close parallel to what medicine calls "the silent killer." Compulsive gambling, however, can't be measured by a blood pressure cuff; it leaves no smell of alcohol and no needle marks—only shattered families and broken lives.

I've been there.

I've lived through my own anger, tears, and loss. As a young man I chased the big winner and came up with empty pockets and a life that teetered on the brink. My gambling addiction actually put four lives on the brink, not just mine. I was given a second chance at life, and I learned how to live without gambling. Finding recovery resurrected my family life and led me to a rewarding career helping gambling addicts and warning others.

I can tell gamblers who feel the noose tightening as their pockets shrink that they are hardly alone with a problem few understand. And all the while, gambling is socially acceptable, heavily promoted, and exploited by government and society.

Most of us grew up with gamblers portrayed as comic and even endearing. We laugh at Nathan Detroit and Sky Masterson in the musical *Guys and Dolls* and at the wit of "Adelaide's Lament." We laugh at the cult classic film *Beat the Devil* when the card players bet on which sugar cube an intruding fly will touch down upon; but they fail to identify which of their buxom companion's breasts the fly will choose to land on first.

Almost all of us have had our harmless brushes with gambling. We buy a scratch-off lottery ticket, go to the two-dollar window at the racetrack, or spend a few days in Las Vegas and write the loss off to entertainment. Some of us even take our kids to Vegas or Atlantic City. We buy a box on the office Super Bowl pool grid, play gin rummy for ten cents a point, or we enjoy an evening of social poker built around table talk and sandwiches. Approximately 95 percent of us can walk away from the table and leave it at that. And 95 percent of us can enjoy wine with dinner or a social drink with friends too. No problem.

But what about the 5 percent or more who are caught in the quicksand of compulsive gambling and don't know how to get out of it? The more they tell themselves they can get out any time they want, the deeper they sink. When they think they've caught a break, or they come into some money and see the light at the end of the tunnel, again they slip up, again they lose, and again they think it can't get any worse.

They are women as well as men. They are young people in college, some of them addicted long before college age. There are some who look in the mirror of their lives and are terrified at what they see. Consider this agonizing, frightened lament of a woman who feels her life and ultimately her family have no escape:

> *I know that it is hard to stop, but I'm not sure how I can be helped.*

It comes down to willpower, and I keep going back. Even though it is destroying me, and I know it is, I don't stop. It is sick. I got to the point of not trying to give it up. Then I don't have to be disappointed in myself for failing to stick to quitting.

It's 11 a.m. and I still haven't played today. But I think about it all morning. It's crazy! There is no life for me outside this because it consumes me and it's scary because I try to stop and always fail.

I want to do this for me and my kids. Why can't I just stop and be done with it? I'm angry with myself and I used to be angry with God, but I know He wants better for me, too. I have not lost anything yet like my home, my kids are great, and I have never gotten in trouble. I want to keep it that way. Do you think it is possible for someone like me to stop? I am thirty-eight and the last four years have been the worst I've experienced.

She wrote that to me, hoping for my help because she couldn't help herself.

Unlike drug addiction, there is no methadone treatment for compulsive gambling. Gamblers, however earnest, are even unlikely to get real help from just reading a book.

This book is not an academic or scholarly study; it's about anger and tears and loss—and redemption. Some people can be saved or rescued. They and those who care about them must first recognize how deep the problem is and how it cuts. I escaped my own dungeon, which included the constant pain of trying to pay debts so my bookmakers would take my next bet. It was as frantic as a cat trying to dig a hole in a marble floor. And the problem has universality.

In some sections of this book, Sheila will explain how my gambling drove her to the edge of life, which we hope will provide understanding to the families of compulsive gamblers. After all, she has lived through all of this right alongside me.

Roughly 13 percent of Gamblers Anonymous (GA) members in the US have attempted suicide, while 48 percent have considered it. In a study of college students in Québec, 7.2 percent of students who did not have a gambling problem had attempted suicide—compared to 26.8 percent of those who were problem gamblers. Suicide attempts are more common with pathological gambling than with any other addiction. And the lures to play are greater now than ever before and get worse every day.

There has always been gambling. Filed dice, the tool of cheats, have been found in ancient pyramids. There have always been card games and dominoes. People have bet that one horse could run faster than another or which fighting rooster could kill another. Surely there was always someone to make book. In our modern society, people bet on sports events in ever more sophisticated and intricate ways. Casino gambling is widespread. States dismiss moral objections to gambling and cleverly tell people they are helping education by buying lottery tickets; forty-three of the fifty states have some form of legalized gambling.

Suicide attempts are more common with pathological gambling than with any other addiction. And the lures to play are greater now than ever before and get worse every day.

"You have to be in it to win it," they say. The promised payoffs are astronomical.

If you win.

Executives of professional sports leagues know their athletes are as vulnerable as anyone to the lure of gambling. They know the history of big-time athletes who sold their will to score to gamblers who controlled which team would win and by how many points. That didn't end with the Black Sox Scandal of 1919 or the basketball scandals of the 1950s. Some of the biggest stars since then have sold out. Sports executives know their games are in jeopardy, but when I have sought to talk to their players, their choice has been to remain silent and hope no one would notice.

Of greater importance are the ordinary young people who fall into the gambling trap and don't recognize it, or tragically don't know that they can get help.

In the late 1990s, a college student at Nassau Community College in New York became overwhelmed by gambling debts. He borrowed and stole all the money he could, but saw no way out. He bought a toy gun, then drove erratically on the Long Island Expressway sideswiping cars. The police gave chase and, when cornered, the student got out of his car, walked toward the police, and drew the realistic looking toy pistol. Police shot and killed him.

When police searched his car they found a suicide note written by the young man that said it was a plan, that he needed to die, and apologized to the police officer who shot him for getting him involved in this "suicide-by-cop."

The harsh reality is that the success rate of treating compulsive gamblers is pathetically less than that of treating drug or alcohol addicts. "That's because we know so little about gambling addiction," says Dr. Allan Lans, who treats drug and alcohol addiction at Smithers in New York and has worked as a counselor for the New York Mets. Our best hope is that we can show the public how bleak the problem is, show people who know a potential addict how deep the addiction is, and encourage them to understand how they might recognize it in time to deal with it.

In the depths of my own addiction and Sheila's suffering, one evening she lay down in front of the door in a plea to keep me from going out to the racetrack.

Without a word, I stepped over her and went anyway.

Eventually, we took our problems, our anger, and our pain to get professional help. We forced ourselves to examine our lives, which by that time were full of recriminations and accusations. And we had some small breakthroughs. We drove together to counseling sessions. Sometimes we even spoke to each other.

Sheila has said, "It began over small things." We learned to communicate about things that seemed trivial, but it was something we were able to do for the first time. If we could have a conversation about the weather, that was a lot for us. If we could have a conversation about where we wanted to go to dinner, that, too, was a big accomplishment. If we could talk through something we were concerned about, or if we could talk to each other about one of the children, that was also a miraculous piece of communication.

Ultimately, I became director of the Council on Compulsive Gambling of New Jersey, and now my wife and I run Arnie & Sheila Wexler Associates, traveling the country presenting workshops and seminars on compulsive gambling addiction. It's hard work and frequently frustrating, as valuable as it is; it's a terribly difficult addiction to break.

And nobody knows better than we do how difficult it is. With help, we managed to escape the problem together, and together we have devoted ourselves to helping others with this addiction we know first-hand.

PROLOGUE

THE MORNING AFTER SUPER Bowl XXI, the hotline phone rings on my desk at the New Jersey Council on Compulsive Gambling. It's Monday, usually the day the bookmaker must be paid. A familiar voice wails to me.

"Arnie! Arnie, I'm a Giants fan and they won everything, and I lost $22,000," the frantic voice says.

"*Geez!*" I say. I'm an experienced man. I've heard a lot of wild stories. I ask, "If you're a Giants fan, how is that possible?"

"I couldn't wait four hours for the final score," the voice laments, "so I bet on the coin toss."

It would be a funny story if it wasn't so sad.

1
♣

WHEELING AND DEALING

IT DIDN'T HAPPEN ALL at once. Actually, it didn't "happen" to me at all; I did it to myself. I make no excuses. Maybe it was in my genes; I always knew I was going to be some kind of compulsive something or other, but there wasn't enough known about compulsive gambling at the time to make that kind of explanation or excuse for me.

Lots of people drink and can control their drinking. They have a social drink or two, or they have wine with dinner or a beer on a hot day after mowing the lawn. They don't become addicted. But a small percentage of them do. People eat every day and most aren't driven to obesity. Most people enjoy a day at the races or bet the Monday night game in the National Football League and don't become compulsive gamblers.

I didn't smoke and I didn't drink. Gambling caught me, and permeated my everyday life. Clearing my desk by the end of each workday was as much a part of my daily routine as going to the track right afterward. I did it every day. I *needed* to do it every day. Maybe that says something about me.

But does that mean the housewife with a compulsion to wipe the kitchen counter a dozen times a day is prone to become a compulsive gambler like me? I wish I knew.

Gambling caught me, and permeated my everyday life. Clearing my desk by the end of each workday was as much a part of my daily routine as going to the track right afterward. I did it every day. I *needed* to do it every day.

I grew up playing pinball machines and, at fourteen, started trading stocks. Playing pinball, I hoped to win a free game. As a kid playing at the boardwalk amusements, nothing gave me more of a high than a pinball machine. I couldn't leave until my money gave out. To this day the sound of a pinball machine juices me up. Trading stocks, another form of gambling, helped me "win" some money. I thought I was so much smarter than other people; it was a challenge to play the market and get away with it. Nobody caught on. It worked for a while, but I got greedy. I was always looking for some play, some action, even back then.

At fourteen is also when I got an after-school job sweeping floors at Harco Dress Co. in New York's Garment District. It gave me pocket money for pinball and fueled my growing fascination with gambling. I started gambling on sports and horses while I was working for fifty cents an hour. My boss told me I better stop or I'd develop a real problem. I laughed at him. I *knew* Arnold Wexler was smart enough to win at gambling. My dream was to be a hotshot salesman and make a lot of money by the time I was thirty. But in a short time I decided that was too slow for me.

One day at work I overheard somebody talking about stock tips, and soon I was wheeling and dealing stocks over the counter. Since economics was my favorite subject in high school, I was a natural. This was way before the stock market became computerized and much more sophisticated. I'd find "pink sheets" in garbage cans and the next morning call a brokerage and say I was Henry Smith or some other person, "from Merrill Lynch." I'd say I wanted to buy 5,000 shares at $2.00 each. Then I'd call back later that day and identify myself as someone else and say I wanted to know what was happening with that stock. If it had gone up, "Henry Smith" would sell. The next day, Henry would buy some other stock and push the price up with other phony buy orders to numerous brokers. I'd manipulate the price up to $5.00, $6.00, or $7.00. Then I'd call the original broker and say I was sending my delivery boy to collect the cash. They never caught on to me.

Nothing ever scared me—or so I thought.

When I was twenty-two I did get arrested, but I was innocent. My boss had sent me to pay a parking ticket for him. I went to court and stayed all morning waiting for the judge to call my boss's name, but the judge called a recess instead. While the court was in recess, I went down to a newsstand, bought a scratch sheet, and went into a phone booth—there were phone booths back in those days—and called my bookmaker.

Suddenly, two guys with strong hands reached in the phone booth and pulled me out by my head. They were New York City detectives. They accused me of being a bookmaker, hustled me into a paddy wagon, and hauled me to the police station in Jamaica, a neighborhood in Queens, and then to a court on Centre Street in Manhattan. They took my fingerprints and mug shot and stuck me in a holding room with a hundred people and a single open toilet in the corner.

That frightened me so much that I was afraid to use the toilet.

I made my one allowed phone call to call my Uncle Ralph, who knew people in Mayor Impellitteri's office. Ralph got me out on $500 bail.

Sheila and I met when I was twenty-one and she was sixteen. As I look back, I had the problem building in me back then, but society didn't consider gambling an addiction at that point, thinking it was a "habit of degenerates." I certainly didn't know what was happening to me. Sheila and I went to the movies on our first date. The next 300 dates were at one racetrack or another, sporting events, or somewhere else where I could gamble.

> I realize today that I needed to gamble like a drug addict needs a high or an alcoholic must have a drink.

Taking her to a racetrack wasn't so simple, though. The first night we went to Monticello Raceway in the Catskill Mountains; she had her hair up in a ponytail and didn't look even sixteen. In those days, the racetracks tried a little harder than today to keep underage kids out. At Monticello, at the first gate we tried, the attendant said Sheila was too young to enter. A couple of other gatekeepers also refused us before we found one who let us in. I had already decided, if they wouldn't let her in, I was going to tell her to wait in the car while I was inside. I was already there. I could smell the action; I surely wasn't going to leave when I was that close, even if she had to wait in the car.

While we dated we set up a joint account to save for our wedding. Sheila put money in, but I wouldn't. I needed my money for gambling.

Not surprisingly, I thought the perfect place for our honeymoon would be Las Vegas or Puerto Rico since both places had casinos, but by that time Sheila didn't think that was a good idea. I suppose she was getting the idea that my gambling was a problem. So we went to Bermuda where we thought there was no gambling.

I was twenty-three when we got married and I thought I could stop gambling if I wanted to. But I was only fooling myself. I'd stop briefly, but I always went back to it. I realize today that I needed to gamble like a drug addict needs a high or an alcoholic must have a drink.

In the lobby of our honeymoon hotel, they had a jar of jellybeans, and if you picked the right number of beans, you won a trip to New York. I already lived in New York, so I didn't have much to gain by winning, but picking jellybeans was action. I spent three days studying the jar of jellybeans and dropping little pieces of paper into the contest box. I didn't win; a guy we met won after he made only one guess, and I was furious. I didn't recognize that counting the jellybeans was a form of gambling.

I can't explain exactly why I married Sheila at the time. I was not in love, to be honest about it. First of all, I didn't know what love was. I went out with two girls before I met Sheila. I was hardly a Don Juan. I was a very shy guy. I lived with my grandparents in New York City and I chose to go to an all-boys high school because I was uncomfortable with girls. In that school setting, I wouldn't have to contend with girls every day. In social situations with girls, I would freeze.

I did have one significant dating experience before I met Sheila: I took a date to Roosevelt Raceway, which was my home turf at that time. I lost money that night and decided that girls were bad luck. When I met Sheila in the Catskills, when I was twenty-one and she was younger at sixteen, I was comfortable with that arrangement.

When gambling owns you, it's the only important thing in your life.

I don't think I had emotional feelings for anything but my gambling back then—not even feeling for myself, and certainly not for anybody else. I never saw affection at home from my mom and dad or between them. When gambling owns you, it's the only important thing in your life. I know I've heard people facing the first stages of their recovery say they had lost the love of their life.

I certainly feel terribly that I disappointed Sheila and hurt her the way I did, but maybe our story together tells the story for a lot of people in love with their addiction.

Four weeks after we were married I went away to the Army Reserve at Fort Dix, New Jersey. For six months, I gambled every day, fast and furious, shooting craps and playing cards in the barracks and running to the phone to bet with my good old bookmaker.

Every waking moment I bet. By the time I came home from the Army in December of 1961, I owed $4,000 and didn't have a job.

When I later went to summer reserve duty at Fort Drum in Watertown, New York, I left a standing bet with my bookmaker for the Mets to win every game and the Yankees to lose every game. That was in the early years of the Mets organization when they lost almost every game they played—that's how nuts I was!

I also left a standing bet on every race ridden by three favored jockeys riding at second-rate tracks around the country. I barely knew the names of those riders. How absurd was that?

I learned that my platoon sergeant was my kind of gambler. So when the rest of the unit was in the barracks or bivouacking in tents at night, he and I stayed at a motel so we could go to Vernon Downs every night.

When I came back to civilian life, the first thing I did was ask my trusted bookmaker, "How did I do?" I couldn't get the daily results from a newspaper at Fort Drum, but all the time I was away I knew at least I had action. I had to have the action, no matter how remote and unseen it was.

I felt a rush of excitement when I knew I had a bet working for me. When I won, I felt great. I felt *so* good. I think that was because I didn't have to run around looking for money to make the next bet and that made it easier for me to feel the high.

> When I won I was high as a kite;
> I had money to bet tomorrow.

Most people who buy those $100 million lottery tickets enjoy a few moments daydreaming about what they'd do if they won: pay off the mortgage, buy a new house, a new car, or a fur coat for the wife, take an exciting vacation trip, make a donation to charity, etc. Not me. Nope. I just thought of paying off gambling debts and having some money left over to bet even more. That was *my* fantasy.

When I won I was high as a kite; I had money to bet tomorrow. One weekend I won $6,000 from my bookmaker. I told him to hold the money because I was going to turn it in to $50,000; if I lost it, I'd have to find more money.

Since I was just a teenager when my gambling began, little did I know it would become a problem. I always thought I was a big shot and could pull off a scam. By the time I was thirty, I was looking for help at the twelve-step program when everyone else there was fifty or sixty years old. I was told I'd never make it because I was too young and hadn't lost enough. But I had already crossed the line to the dream world of addiction. I had been building my addiction since I was seven years old.

So far I've talked a lot about how life was as a gambler, but I couldn't have done it alone. Sheila came along for the ride, and throughout this book she offers her take on what it was like living with me, being married to me, and the many financial problems we experienced, before I quit the bet.

SHEILA'S EXPERIENCE

I was sixteen years old in the summer of 1958 when Arnie came along. It must have been love at first sight, and it was like a sweet scene out of the film *Dirty Dancing*. We met in rowboats at Avon Lodge, a summer resort bungalow colony in the Catskill Mountains, where New York families escaped the stifling heat of the city.

I was rowing a boat in the lake with a friend from the bungalow colony and Arnie was rowing one, too. My friend said he was a nice guy and we went over and bumped his boat on purpose. It was as charming as Hollywood could make it. I'd go with friends or my family to see the entertainment, the comedians, the singers, or the dancers that the lodge would present after dinner. The Catskills had some great entertainers. Arnie would be at the pinball machines instead. He loved to play them.

Everyone would say, "You want to find Arnie? He's at the pinball machines." It was a standing joke, but I didn't mind; we'd just get together later in the evening. Someone who has been around gamblers could say the signs were there, and surely I can say that now, but what did I know? My father played gin rummy with the guys once a week, and that had been my only exposure to any form of gambling.

On my first date with Arnie, we went to see *Damn Yankees* at a drive-in at South Fallsburg, the next town over. Our second date was at Monticello Raceway, and I never had another date with him unless it was a sports event, a racetrack, or a casino night—except for an occasional Broadway show. He was as charming as the gamblers are in *Guys and Dolls*.

I was painfully shy and here came this outgoing, loveable guy. Everyone who knew him loved him. He was even nice to my grandmother. He was generous and it seemed he always had a few dollars in his pocket. I saw those things and I decided the other stuff was incidental. He says he understands now that he was "bullshitting" people to cover up his own insecurity, but I never saw that.

It was fun at the track with him. He taught me how to make a "show" bet—bet a horse to finish third or better—a cautious beginner's bet. I would jump up and down like a lunatic for my $2 bet. What I didn't see was that while I was placing my little bet, he was betting big money. At times, I would get a knot in my stomach because he would get crazy, screaming and yelling and cursing at the driver or the jockey and banging on the fence, even though he had been the nicest, softest guy I had ever met. I never saw that side of him except at the track and I'd shrug it off. I had no idea about problem gambling; I was in love.

I was seventeen when we became engaged. My grandmother gave Arnie her stone so he could give me a ring.

When we were dating he did things I thought were so endearing. One time I was at Avon Lodge for the summer while Arnie worked in North Bergen, New Jersey. He'd leave North Bergen after work and I'd find him in the morning at the resort, sleeping in his car with his feet sticking out. What I didn't know was that he was losing his money at the harnesstrack before coming to Avon and wasn't going to waste any more on a $6 motel room.

He was often late picking me up for dates at home and one time he didn't show up at all. One time he was in jail on suspicion of bookmaking. His mother covered for him, every time I phoned her, by telling me that he was in the shower. I said, "Ma, how many showers can he take?"

There were signs Arnie had a gambling problem, but I didn't see them yet—or I refused to see them. I hope today that parents and young people are more educated about addiction than I was, and the signs they should recognize. The signs should have scared me off. He admitted to me that he owed a lot of money and explained that his father had died at the age of twenty-six, and so he was going to make a lot of money for me in case he died young.

He gambled like crazy; he was determined to get rich quick. But he said he could quit any time he wanted. And he became so withdrawn sometimes I was afraid he wanted to back out of marrying me. I was happy about getting married, as were so many girls my age in those days.

We were both working at the time, and set up a savings account for furniture and curtains and other things we'd need when we got married. But when we went to get the money out after the wedding, I found out Arnie had never put his share in.

He told me about the money he owed. To me it was a fortune. A bookmaker friend of his told me I needed to give Arnie a choice between me and gambling—one or the other— so I got up my courage and actually told him that. He said he loved me and once we got married he was never going to make another bet. I believed him.

Looking back, Arnie's sister, who had seen his gambling fixation grow from the beginning, also told me to get out. His grandmother warned me to watch out, too.

I felt bad for the childhood he'd had—his father died when Arnie was just two years old and he had issues with his

11

stepfather—and I thought that was the root of his problem. I felt sorry for him. I thought that with my help he'd be okay, that I could save him, but I couldn't. Love is blind and stupid, too.

I think back to when I was a kid, to a time before I met Arnie. I grew up in the Bronx as an only child. My father was a postal worker and he always worked a second job and sometimes a third so we could escape to the Catskills in the summer. My mother was sickly and I was more the caretaker of her than she was of me. I was going to the High School of Music and Art in New York City, and had hopes of going on to Julliard and becoming a music teacher. A friend of the family had promised to pay for me if I went there.

I thought that with my help he'd be okay, that I could save him, but I couldn't.

What I understand now is that I was waiting for someone I could fix. It was a setup from my early years: I was always in the role of worrying about someone and trying to help them. Nowadays they call it codependency.

We had a Saturday night wedding at the Concourse Plaza Hotel in the Bronx, which was a really nice hotel. But we had all these wedding gifts and Arnie wouldn't leave the reception room until all the envelopes were opened. He was looking for cash. So most of my wedding night was spent opening envelopes and looking for money.

He wanted to honeymoon in Las Vegas or Puerto Rico. They had gambling there. I thought that was *not* a good idea. We decided we were going to Bermuda instead.

In Bermuda, he was very uneasy and that made me nervous that something was wrong. That was when he found the jar of jellybeans on the hotel registration desk. Sounded like a sugar high was the greatest danger, but Arnie found it was a way to get the gambling high he craved. If you guessed the number of jellybeans, you won a trip to New York, but the prize wasn't what he was playing for. We were already from New York. He spent much of our three days studying the bowl, guessing, writing numbers on pieces of paper, and dropping them in a box on the desk. It was action and he needed his fix.

I remember how he promised he wouldn't gamble once we were married, so I guess he thought it would be okay beforehand. He couldn't say to himself that he was addicted to gambling, but he had made his promise and I believe he really wanted to quit.

While we were still on our honeymoon, a horse he had unsuccessfully bet on twice in the weeks before our wedding was set to run in the Belmont. Arnie had all the facts and figures in his head. A horse named Carry Back had won the Derby and the Preakness and would surely be a big favorite to win the Belmont and complete the Triple Crown. If any horse could beat him, the payoff would surely be great, and Arnie still liked Sherluck, the horse he'd been betting on. To Arnie, "Sherl" meant Sheila and "luck" meant just what it said. How could he lose?

If he hadn't made that promise to me to quit gambling, he would have bet $600 on the Belmont because that's how he gambled—the $200 lost in the Derby plus the $400 he lost in the Preakness meant $600 would have been bet on the Belmont.

Well, Arnie kept his promise to me and didn't place the bet, but Sherluck won in a great upset and paid the largest price in Belmont history to that point—$132.20 for a $2 bet. Arnie saw that his winning bet would have been worth $40,000, and he was furious. It was *my* fault he didn't win, he said. Look what I did to him. Why did he get married?

We had a terrible fight and I made him go out on the balcony with me so the chambermaid wouldn't see us. I was so humiliated. That was the end of my honeymoon.

I was married to this man and gambling was more important to him than I was. Yes, the honeymoon was over, before it had barely begun.

In my heart, though, I was still clinging to a newlywed's dream. I was married and I liked the idea. I felt like I was still a kid with my boyfriend, and I was looking forward to living the daydream of playing house, doing things together, doing new things, doing things I liked—making a home for us far and away from my parents' house.

But two weeks after we were married, the circumstance of loving and being married to a gambling addict came home to roost. We had postponed buying furniture and moving into an apartment together because Arnie had been drafted into the Army Reserves and was scheduled to go away for six months of active duty. For a while, we stayed together at a guest hotel in Queens, New York, and when he was inducted into the service I went to live with my mother and father. He wasn't so far away at Fort Dix, New Jersey. I anticipated being back together with Arnie after those six months and really living as husband and wife.

We put a deposit down on an apartment that became available a couple of weeks before he was discharged from the Army. With our wedding gift money, we had picked out $1,200 of furniture and the store was holding it all on deposit. I was really excited about fixing up the apartment and assumed we would use our wedding gifts to do it.

I was raised to think that the man was head of the household, so Arnie managed all the finances even in those first months of our marriage. When he was about to come home from the Army, I went to get money from the bank so I could have the furniture delivered. Somehow the wedding money wasn't there; I was absolutely stunned and couldn't understand. The only thing I did understand was that things were not going as planned. It wasn't going to be such a smooth reunion when Arnie came home. I think I was too bewildered to even cry.

He had gambled away everything we had saved. We had to borrow from his grandmother to get started. He claimed he played cards a lot in the barracks because he was bored and he missed me. Of course, that touched me; what a foolish romantic I was. But instead of having the money to set up a home, he returned to civilian life in December 1961, married, owing $4,000, and having no job. He told me he had to take out a loan. He cried. He was so remorseful. I believed him.

Not only were we already in debt, but I had my first demonstration of what a creative liar I was married to. It wasn't until years later that I recognized just *how creative* he was. Those were crocodile tears. He told me all the guys in the Army "screw around with broads" or cheat on their wives while they're apart, or are out at night drinking. He wasn't doing that. So he made himself out to be the good guy. What he did was gamble. That's all.

He told me he gambled because he missed me so much and that gambling was filling the void in his life. He assured me that out-of-control gambling was never going to happen again.

2

♦

CRAFT AND GRAFT

How did I do it?

How was I able to finance my compulsion as I got deeper and deeper in the hole? I was very smart, that's how. And I was a highly creative liar. Researchers and psychologists—smarter than I am—say that's how compulsive gamblers are. We're highly creative liars.

I was also devious and dishonest, which is how compulsive gamblers manage to fool everyone initially. It really has nothing to do with morality. I think I'm a moral person. Of course, my attitude about myself today is practically a whole lifetime after my last bet.

I had to have money to feed my gambling, so I took it, I found it, or I stole it. Wherever and whenever I could take it, I did. The fact that I was good at my job and nobody could smell on my breath the bets I lost made that possible. The great irony is that in spite of all of this, I got promoted to a big deal position because the man who held the job before me was fired for stealing.

I had to have money to feed my gambling, so I took it, I found it, or I stole it.

After Sheila and I got married, I left the Army and started making $60 a week as a salesman for Jonathan Logan Dresses and had use of a company car. The executives liked me, and the number two guy in the company *really* liked me.

I'd worked as a salesman for almost a year when they found out that the guy running their cutting, sewing, and shipping operations in North Bergen, New Jersey was stealing from them. They offered me $125 a week to take his job.

The promotion made me feel like I was in heaven. The big boss, David Schwartz, was doing $6 to $10 million in business a year from his office in Manhattan, and I was running the plant in New Jersey across the George Washington Bridge that spanned the Hudson River. I was supervising 400 or 500 people, but had two assistant managers doing most of the work, so I was free to run around the plant borrowing from everyone I could to sustain my cash flow, or "betting fuel."

I'd wake up in the morning thinking I would go to the track and win every bet. Or I'd call my bookmaker and bet every game on his line for college basketball or football, thinking I'd win forty out of forty-two bets. I can't tell you even where some of the schools were—Slippery Rock or Pepperdine or some other school I'd never heard of. I didn't care. It was action and that was all that mattered. My bookie always took my action.

I thought I was an expert on baseball. In football, I couldn't name three players. In hockey, I never saw a game—I didn't even know it was played on ice. But I always bet.

That was in the early years of the American Football League (AFL), before it was absorbed into the National Football League (NFL) in the 1970 merger. My bookmaker didn't have a line on AFL games, but I was such a good customer that he told me to make my own line. But I still couldn't win.

Then the good money I was making at Jonathan Logan wasn't quite good enough.

At times, when I had lost just about all I had, I'd drive to the racetrack with $6 in my pocket and park my car in a rush without paying attention to where I parked it. I was just in time to bet the little money I had left on the daily double. On those occasions when I'd win, it was like I had found the end of the rainbow. Then I'd scramble around in the dark parking lot trying to find my car.

Other times I'd rush after work to the trotters at Roosevelt Raceway on Long Island, stopping just long enough for a bowl of Chinese soup at Gam Wah's. I couldn't afford the money or the time to order more than just soup. I'd tip the waiter a quarter, which was generous in those days. I was good that way. It was a wonder how I ever had money to buy gas for the car.

I was also keeping the games running at work, in the sense that I was making it look like I was actually running the plant as I'd been hired to. In fact, since the two assistant managers kept things running so smoothly for me, the only time I wasn't on the phone gambling was when I was showing a customer around the plant. Mr. Schwartz would make his periodic management trips to check on the factory, and he had an image as a tough guy. I gave the girl at the switchboard in the New York office $20 a week to give me a warning call when the boss left to come to the plant so I could get it into business mode. When he came by, everybody would be hard at work. I'd stand up in the aisle and was the only person he could talk to. I wasn't afraid of him. He liked that.

After about six months, he told me he had a nice girl for me. Since Sheila and I were married, I said, "Thanks, but I don't need social help." But he had me write down my name for him. A week later he offered me 500 shares of Jonathan Logan stock, which were selling at $8 each. Nobody else in the plant got that offer, but I took it. He told me "go make a baby" and I'd get a raise. I made a daughter and he gave me a raise. Then the stock that was selling for $8 a share went to $78. As it rose, I'd take more and more of it on margin. Buying on margin was risky, but I didn't care. Soon I had taken almost all of the money out of the stocks and lost it gambling. I wince at the recollection of how much higher the stock went. But my needs were immediate.

Of the nearly 500 people working in the plant, a lot of them were gamblers, too. In the plant, I set up a room where guys could gamble over lunch. They called it the Goulash Room. Sometimes I'd bring sandwiches while they shot craps and played cards. Unless I got a warning call that the boss was coming, I gambled or organized ways to make Jonathan Logan Dresses work for me. For example, I was getting bonus graft from retail dress stores for letting them into the plant and giving them first pick of the merchandise.

I'd also know when some "special" customers had favorite teams they liked to bet: the Yankees, Giants, or Knicks, for example. My bookmaker had me make a split-line for those special customers and I'd make the odds for their bets three points higher. For myself, I'd bet the middle.

When Jonathan Logan dresses weren't moving, they had to be "unloaded"—sold at a loss—and I set the prices. If a dress was marked down to $29, I'd deliver it to some shops at $19 per dress on paper, and I'd keep the $10 difference for myself. Nobody caught on to my scam.

Anybody selling me boxes or hangers gave me a kickback. The guy handling our airfreight gave me $100 every week. I was taking dresses off the line, selling them to selected customers and pocketing the money. I'd tell a truck driver I had a dress for his wife at a good price.

Though I was crafty, at one point I owed $16,000 to my bookmaker and he was pushing me to pay off my debt. He threatened to stop taking my action, which got my attention. So I made a deal with his brother and partner, "Pete, the Loan Shark," to steer people from the plant to him to take their bets. I'd get 25 percent of their losses if they placed bets with him.

Every Monday—when I could—I'd straighten out my wins and losses and make good with my bookmaker. In those days, the bookmaker and his clients were almost like friends in the neighborhood. We'd see each other at parties and bar mitzvahs and other social events.

In November of 1967, I bet $3,600 on three NFL games I liked very much. That was $10,800 I couldn't possibly pay off if I lost. The bookmaker said, "Arnie, don't jerk me around." If we'd lost the phone connection, I couldn't have called him back because I didn't have money for the call. He said I couldn't bet with him anymore if I lost the bets and couldn't pay. That was a worse threat than losing the money. Fortunately, I won two of the three games. If I had lost, I didn't know how I was going to pay. In my mind, I just thought I'd steal more dresses. Nothing mattered; I could always get money.

All I wanted was an edge,
a hint about the winner.

One day a guy came into the plant to sell boxes and I asked for a cut. He said he couldn't do that, but that he had great information at Roosevelt Raceway. He was a former major league baseball player. That sounded so good to me, I could taste it; with information like that, I would be smarter than the odds-makers. This fellow said he was betting for some of the drivers. For years, there had been talk about fixed harness races. It looked so easy for a driver to tug the reins and hold his horse back enough to finish second or third and let another horse win.

All I wanted was an edge, a hint about the winner. I would be as good as gold. This was a dream come true. A driver wearing a straw hat would come over to where the box salesman was sitting in the clubhouse and give him an envelope with a program marked with which horses to bet. I would be sitting next to him. I was a kid betting across the board, and at the end of the week I won $2,000. We both made a lot of money before the envelope exchange had to stop when our source was told to take his horses out of New York. Many years later, a driver known as "the Babe Ruth of harness racing" was suspended for five years after being implicated in a fixing scandal. I guess a lot of other people had that same idea, too.

Unfortunately, I couldn't limit my betting to just that simple dream-come-true. Not while there were still basketball and football games to be bet. Compulsive gamblers know no boundaries and have no off-season.

With the graft I was running on Jonathan Logan Dresses and some gambling successes supplementing my salary, I was making $50,000 a year—a lot of cash in those days—but by the end of the year, I didn't have a nickel.

I used to come home from the track and go to bed crying like a baby. I swore I was never going to bet again. There were nights when I would pray that I wouldn't wake up in the morning. But the next morning I'd wake up, buy a racing form, and believe that was going to be the day I would finally sweep the boards on everything I bet.

Years later when I was a counselor, a guy who was in a twelve-step program won a ton of money in the lottery and became instantly famous. Now he's broke—he lost the money, lost everything. Money to a gambling addict is all about more money, not about buying a fur coat or a Rolls Royce or paying a mortgage.

Compulsive gamblers know no boundaries and have no off-season.

SHEILA'S EXPERIENCE

It took years for things to get as bad for us as they finally did.

Arnie got a job a few months after he left the Army. He could hold down a job and get promoted for doing it well despite his gambling.

One night a week he played cards; that was fine with me because once a week I played Canasta or Mahjong. We were both working and had limited time for a social life. He didn't like friends of mine unless they gambled, unless they played cards or went to the track or something.

We went to his mother's house on Sundays and my mom's house one night a week—typical newlywed stuff. I would cook at home but we rarely had dinner together. Chances were, when we did, we'd have a fight. I thought it was the pressure of him going to work on Monday, but actually he was uptight because that was the day he had to settle with his bookmaker.

We lived in a nice apartment complex in the Woodside part of Queens and in the beginning I could accept that it was furnished with hand-me-downs and used stuff that people were throwing out or giving away. I know a lot of young newlyweds do that in the beginning while they're saving money, so it didn't bother me a great deal.

On Saturday afternoons, when Arnie wasn't working, I'd ask him what he wanted to do that evening. We always ended up going to the track—to Roosevelt Raceway or Yonkers if we were home, or to Monticello if we were away in the mountains. We'd have seats in the clubhouse for dinner and to bet on the horses. I'd always order the cheapest things on the menu. I really didn't care for it there; I always felt it was sleazy.

I'd pick a horse because of its name or I liked the color of the rider's shirt and I'd bet $2 to show. Arnie would say he needed to go to the bathroom or he needed to buy peanuts or ice cream or something and disappear for a while. What I later learned was that was his excuse to go to the window to bet $50 or $100, or sometimes to cash a winning ticket.

It was like that when we went to the movies, when he'd say he had to go to the bathroom so he really could phone his bookmaker or listen to the baseball scores on a transistor radio. I didn't know he was betting other sports besides the races. He'd also phone the bookmaker from the house. When I overheard his phone calls, I didn't understand what they were talking about or I didn't realize just how much he was betting.

The bookmaker would name the teams on his end of the line and Arnie would say either "yes" or "no." The same thing happened with bets I thought were $2. The bookmaker would say $100, $200, $300, and Arnie would say either "yes" or "no." That's all I would hear. Arnie kept me in the dark.

The debts and financial losses kept coming.

My obligation, as I saw it, was to help him and sacrifice where I could. It was a time in our society when a wife was brought up to feel obligated to support her husband for better or for worse. Wives stood by their husbands. So it was *we* who owed four grand, like when he first got home from the Army, not just Arnie. That's just the way it was, and this became a continuing cycle for us; we were always paying off loans.

I was commuting to work from Queens to Wall Street making $98 a week at an insurance company as a calculating clerk with actuarial formulas. I began brown-bagging it, taking lunch to work, instead of going to the cafeteria, I didn't get my hair done, and made whatever other sacrifices I had to make to get us out of debt. Whatever money I made went to Arnie to pay the bills.

I was looking forward to paying off the loans, and each time I figured out a date in my mind when it was going to be over, whenever we'd get close, I would mark the date on the calendar when the loan would be paid off. I believed we were on our way to digging ourselves out of the hole.

But a month or so before the planned payoff date, Arnie would have a meltdown when he would cry and tell me he was so sorry and that the loan was not going to be paid off. He said he had to refinance and we had to repay the loan again for that many more months. A lot of sick feelings in my stomach were on those calendars.

We were always in financial straits, and I was in denial. He said he would come up with some kind of solution, but it always meant sacrificing more. He told me he would quit, that he would make more money, and I wanted to believe him. But that never happened.

My dream of a happy married life became my nightmare, but still I loved Arnie. I still can't believe what we went through because of his gambling. Then again, you never know what you're capable of or what you're willing to do for someone you love. That's just the way it is.

By now, we were living in a shabby apartment in Kew Gardens, Queens, a neighborhood of New York City. It was still furnished with hand-me-downs from his family or mine, or with furniture I bought from my hairdresser. Later on we got one of the kids' beds when his grandfather died. Rather than face the pain of reality, I would walk around the apartment nursing a daydream. I'd tell myself, "When we move, I'm going to paint the kitchen yellow. I'm not going to take this dining room set; we're going to get a new set." I'd walk into each room and say what I was going to do, what the kids' rooms' colors were going to be, and I would fantasize.

Then I'd tell my neighbor next door that Arnie decided we weren't going to buy a house this year because it wasn't the right time to buy—but we definitely would next spring and probably wouldn't sign a lease for next year. I'd live on that idea. Now, though, I don't think either the neighbor or I believed it.

We were married about two years or so when Dave Schwartz, who owned Jonathan Logan Dresses where Arnie worked, took a liking to my husband. The owner was a tyrant, and whenever he walked into the factory Arnie didn't know any better so he and the boss would have a conversation. Before he learned Arnie was married, he would say he had a girl for him. One day he asked for Arnie's name and address and soon offered him chance to buy a stock option on 500 shares. I didn't know what a stock option was. Arnie jumped at the offer. For 500 shares of stock, we borrowed $7,200, and it grew to be worth $39,000 in a relatively short time. In the mid-'60s, you could buy a new car for $2,000, so this was an enormous amount of money. I had more money in my hands than ever before in my life. Or so I thought.

He blew it all, like he always did.

I didn't know at the time, but Arnie was selling the stock bit by bit to pay for his gambling debts until there was nothing left. I found out when I got a letter about the stock from the brokerage house that there were fifty shares left. I called Arnie to tell him.

I don't know if I ever had confidence in myself, but whatever confidence I might have had was gone. I'd phone him at work and he'd always be ready with an explanation; whatever excuse he made up, I believed him. He said someone with his same name lived in his mother's building, which I knew was true. That must be the mistake, he said; he'd call the broker and straighten it out. Then he would tell me that he called and made the correction.

Another time a letter came from the bank that Arnie couldn't have the new loan he requested because he had too much outstanding debt. I didn't know we had any outstanding debt and I didn't know he was looking to borrow more money. I phoned him about that. He said it wasn't a loan for us; it was for Michael, a friend of Arnie's, who needed it in a hurry. Michael was a good friend and I knew he was also a gambler. This was the first time I had the nerve to tell Arnie that I didn't believe him. I said I knew he was lying, so he brought Michael home to prove I was wrong. I told them they should leave the house right then and there because I knew it was all a lie.

Another time he said he was taking a loan for Joe, who was newly married, and if Joe's wife found out he'd been gambling she was going to leave him. I couldn't let that happen. Joe was thirty years old and I liked him very much. I said "sure," and every week Arnie would come home with a crisp $100 bill and put it in on the table. Actually, it turned out Joe and Arnie were partners in a bookmaking operation at the time and sharing the money, but Arnie was betting and losing more with other bookmakers than he was making with Joe. He'd give me this $100 bill to put in the drawer until Monday and said he would pay Household Finance Company. Of course, when the time came, HFC never got paid. And the loan wasn't for Joe. Arnie and his gambling buddies, it seemed, came before me. But I loved Arnie, so I always went along.

And another time he borrowed $3,000 from his boss, who would take money out of Arnie's check every week to pay it back. We'd been married seven years before I caught on as to why he wasn't bringing home what he was supposed to. Arnie didn't get the raise he told me he was promised, he'd tell me, or everybody else got the Christmas bonus, but he didn't. Then he'd say he couldn't bring his paycheck home because now the company was paying in cash. But he was bringing home envelopes with all the deductions itemized; I wasn't *that* stupid.

He was working with hundreds of people in North Bergen, and they were paying him cash? It didn't make sense. What did they do? Did they bring a Brink's truck full of cash to the plant on Friday afternoon? And he would give me only $10 to run the house. It was crazy.

I got suspicious and decided I'd figure things out from his W2 from the year before. By now, I was doubting whether I was even capable of adding up numbers. When I would squeeze him about my numbers, he'd take a sheet of paper and start writing his numbers very fast. He'd circle a number, write it on one side of the paper, and circle it again. He'd put together a sheet that was so confusing that I would give up, which he knew I would.

By now, I was doubting whether I was even capable of adding up numbers.

So, I did the W2 review again and found out it was short $25 a week. Then I did what I always did: I called him at work and I said, "I found out you're lying to me." He said that was so easy to explain, but he was in a meeting and when he got home he'd explain.

He came home and explained that he worked in New Jersey and we lived in New York, and therefore there was a different tax system. He showed me the numbers and the difference was precisely $25 a week. One Friday evening he had the name and number of someone from the IRS office in Jamaica, New York, and I could call on Monday and that guy would explain the difference. Arnie knew I'd never make the call, so he was safe. I knew at that point he wasn't telling the truth, but I didn't know how to confront him.

Love is blind and sometimes it's deaf too. I just wasn't listening. I got letters and phone calls, and if I pursued them I could have found out some of the truth, but I never did. I'd cry all the time. Sometimes I'd cry all night long. Arnie doesn't remember seeing me cry, but I'd wake him to show him that I had. I used to shake him in his sleep and say, "Look at what you're doing to me." I'd want him to *see* what he was doing to me.

3

♠

BOTTOMLESS QUICKSAND

I READ ONCE THAT a high-brow is a man who has found something more interesting than women. I don't think he was talking about preferring to bet the horses or play galloping dominoes to sex. But when I had a good day betting, I was so high I didn't need sex. If I was having a bad day and lost, I didn't want anything less. Sometimes when we did have sex, Sheila would ask me, "Do you hear a radio?" Of course, I would tell her she was crazy, but I did have a radio on under the pillow so I could listen to a game. That was my life.

Not surprisingly, Sheila and I had started fighting all the time about anything and everything. We loved each other and hated each other at the same time.

I can hardly believe what a rat I was, but especially to Sheila. In the desperation stage of my disease, I'd lose and didn't feel it; I'd win and didn't feel it. After a win, the only thing I'd feel is that I had money to bet tomorrow. So for that moment I didn't have to worry about borrowing or stealing—or Sheila. I had action for tomorrow.

I couldn't even care about myself. The only thing I cared about was making a bet.

One morning when Sheila's first pregnancy was coming to term, I told her I was going to work, and she asked what to do if she needed to go to the hospital. I told her to call my brother because I was busy at work. She didn't know until years later that I went to the track. What a guy I was.

Another time, Sheila was going through a difficult subsequent pregnancy and my gambling was worsening. I took her to the hospital in the middle of the night and left her in a medication room because they didn't have a patient room available.

The next morning I called my boss and told him I couldn't come to work because my wife was in the hospital. I went home and made the phone calls I needed to make to the bookie. Then I went to the racetrack. At five o'clock in the evening—after spending the day at the track—I went to see how Sheila was doing.

The doctor told me Sheila was in shock, had almost died, and had lost the baby. But I really didn't care about her, the loss of the baby, or our other two kids. By then, I couldn't even care about myself. The only thing I cared about was making a bet. I had no money and couldn't wait to lose even more.

My wife had suffered through an excruciating miscarriage, and, though I feel terribly guilty about it now, at the time I was thinking that if she had died, it would have solved all my problems. I wouldn't have had to tell her how bad things were. I was trapped in my gambling and didn't think I could change things. Gambling had become the core of my life.

After that first meeting, I still thought I was just on a losing streak and really wasn't a compulsive gambler.

I owed everybody and his brother a lot of money. I thought I would never ever stop gambling. When I stopped, I owed more than three times my yearly pay and thought about killing myself every day. I saw suicide as the only way out. At least I could leave Sheila the $5,000 insurance policy I had.

Then I got a new boss at work—his name was Jerry. I heard he had a lot of money so I saw another bailout. After I worked for him for six months, I asked him to give me, or loan me, some money. He told me I had a gambling problem, needed help, and that I should go to a twelve-step program. He said, "They will help you out with the money you owe." I thought he meant they would pay off my gambling debts. So I went to the twelve-step meeting having no idea that they *wouldn't* pay off my debts or give me money. I didn't want to stop; I was just looking for a bailout.

Three days after we talked, Jerry was fired. But I went to the twelve-step meeting as he had suggested. After that first meeting, I still thought I was just on a losing streak and really wasn't a compulsive gambler. But I did stop and that date, the date of my last bet, was April 10, 1968.

Although April 10, 1968 was the last bet I made, I still had doubts that I was a compulsive gambler. Even though I did not gamble again, I had urges. On September 26, 1968, I went to Greenhaven Prison for a gamblers' twelve-step meeting. I was in the waiting room with lots of people coming to visit. I saw husbands in jail kissing their kids and wives through wire fences, and then in the meeting I saw some of the same guys.

I started to think about all the things I did that could have put me in prison with them. That day changed my thinking; how lucky I was that I never got caught. On the way home, we talked in the car, and when we got home, Sheila, my friend, his wife, and I stayed up talking until 4:00 a.m.

That was when it all clicked. After that day, I never thought, *Gee I am not a compulsive gambler*. That was over forty-six years ago but I remember it like it was yesterday.

I didn't see Jerry again until Sheila and I were out one day walking in New York City. At point, I hadn't placed a bet in ten years. Jerry attended my tenth anniversary celebration.

Sometime back, at a meeting on the subject of gamblers and alcoholics—I attend lots of these meetings—a highly-regarded expert said that addicts have a total recall of the bad things that happen to them, but not the good things. Bull! I can remember my first big winner and it's a lifetime ago. Every time you get a big win, it stays in your head.

Even when you're in the desperation phase, you can have a big win and you think, *Jesus, that could happen again!* It's like a drug addict getting a hit of whatever. It's like having the best sex of your life and you think, *Wow, I'd like to have that again!* And you chase that feeling the rest of your life. In my case, a big win was always better than sex.

Of course, I loved Sheila. I must have loved her; I'm seventy-six years old and we're still married, and we even work together. She must have loved me all the while because she stuck with me all those years when I made life so difficult for her; although I don't know how or why she stayed. It's been fifty-two years of marriage—seven years of garbage followed by forty-six years of good times since I quit the bet. I can review my past this way, from an informed perspective that has evolved over time, and in a way I never could have if I hadn't been able to finally face the depths of my addiction and get help.

Even when you're in the desperation phase, you can have a big win and you think, *Jesus, that could happen again!* It's like a drug addict getting a hit of whatever. It's like having the best sex of your life and you think, *Wow, I'd like to have that again!* And you chase that feeling the rest of your life.

The way I see it, I'm now a *recovering* compulsive gambler. It's a progressive disease, hidden until the sufferer ultimately recognizes that he is suffering in a way that consumes his life and makes him cheat and lie in a way he would never have considered. Compulsive gamblers even believe their own lies. Some will steal and go to jail. Some will die from the stress they've inflicted on themselves. Some will opt for suicide as a way out.

Now for many years I have been trying to help people escape the bottomless quicksand of gambling addiction. I try to give those who are addicted a rope so they can grab on and crawl out of the pit. A small number will seek real help. Some will get their head straight again. It's a demanding effort. I know I help some get through the change; often I fail.

Gambling is a different kind of addiction. I'd like to call it a *curse*, except it's hard for me not to blame myself. So many people don't understand the hold it has and can't recognize it. People around me couldn't smell it on my breath. I didn't nod off at work. There were no track marks on my arms. There is no blood test or urine test for my kind of addiction. I could hide it.

Responsible loan officers must not have recognized my problem because they kept loaning me money I couldn't repay. I couldn't even acknowledge what I was for so long. But eventually, deep inside, I knew I had a serious problem.

Until I reached the very bottom of the pit I was free-falling into and experienced an awakening, I couldn't admit to myself how gambling had taken over my life or how I had finally reached the point of complete desperation and disaster.

I understand that no compulsive gambler gets out of trouble by reading a book any more than problem drinkers or drug users do, but I hope that somehow I can be a warning sign for others who feel that it *can't*, that it *won't,* happen to them or their family members. More realistically, I hope to draw a picture so people who laugh at the gamblers in *Guys and Dolls* can understand how real the problem is, and how awful it can be for those who love a compulsive gambler.

Obviously, I found a way out because I'm writing this book and am a functioning family man today. But I hope you can understand how crushing the problem was and how excruciating it was to get out from under it. If you saw Frank Sinatra writhe and sweat in the film *The Man with the Golden Arm* as he fought his heroin addiction, you get the idea—except that fighting gambling takes longer. When the former gambler in the senior citizens' center picks up a deck in a friendly gin game, the rush of adrenaline comes back. He or she thinks about the bet.

Today, having been through the journey of successful treatment, I feel some guilt, but I have greater pride in the fact that I haven't looked back since the worst of those days, when I decided—with Sheila's support—that I had to stop to save my life. I wonder, while I wandered through the fog, how I felt about myself. But I think that wasn't part of the equation.

How do drug addicts feel about themselves at the beginning of their disease? If they knew what they were doing to themselves, it might be much easier for them to break their habits. What they know for sure is that they feel good when they're high. I don't think they want to look deep inside themselves while they are getting high. That's my opinion.

SHEILA'S EXPERIENCE

Arnie wasn't interested in making love. I'd say I heard a radio and he'd say it must be in the next apartment. He'd put the transistor radio under the pillow so he could get the scores. Sometimes I'd wake up and look over and I'd be alone in bed. He'd be out in the car in another neighborhood where he knew he could get out-of-town scores. I'd think he had left me and I'd cry until he came home.

On weekends, he would never leave the house before he phoned the bookmaker, who opened his office at 11:30 a.m. We'd be invited to a friend's home at two o'clock in the afternoon and Arnie would insist we get there at one o'clock so he could watch the ball game. When we visited friends at night, he'd insist they have a TV to watch the game. Five or six people would be in one room having a good time and he would watch the game, alone, in another room. When everyone was getting ready to leave, he'd make sure we were in the car in time to hear the sports results. We'd argue about a lot of things. Sometimes he'd pick a fight just so he could leave the house to listen to scores.

Most often we'd argue about money. We never had any. I got a look at the loan book. I wasn't sure if he was paying on it or not.

The pressure from the bookmaker was so great that one Monday he told Arnie if he didn't bring the money he couldn't bet the game that night. That, I learned, was the greatest of threats—to cut Arnie off. So Arnie sold our year-old blue Impala with only 10,000 miles on it for $500.

Our landlord was turning the apartments into a co-op and we had to come up with $1,500 to hold our unit. We didn't have the money, so we moved. I thought I might be pregnant, so I told my friends I wanted to be closer to my mother, that I was sure it would be cheaper where we were moving to, and I thought I could use my father's car.

Sometimes Arnie would win $1,000, come home, and give me $100 to go buy something for myself or for the kids. Mostly he'd give me $25 or so because that was all he could spare from his gambling money. A big win was money used for gambling and nothing else. He thought that he was on a lucky streak and would have the money to gamble again the next day. It was his ego talking when he won big and ran around the factory the next day telling everybody. But I never heard him tell everybody about all the money he lost.

At home, he'd be in a bright mood, but it didn't last long because he knew that the next day he might take a hit. I'd ask myself why he didn't talk to me or pay attention to me and why he often didn't come home when he was supposed to. We were living in the apartment like two single people. We were like complete strangers sharing a common space.

Now he says he was afraid to talk to me because I had questions he couldn't answer, or he felt he had to lie. He was growing short-tempered and moody. I felt that he didn't love me and I tried to make him prove he did. One time I said the house was on fire as a test to see if he was listening. He went right on gambling. He never paused.

I would cry for hours before he came home and I'd look in the mirror to make sure I looked like I had been crying. He might ask me "What's the matter?" Or else he didn't come home or didn't ask me. Maybe I should have walked out, but I didn't.

Periodically a bomb would drop. Two years after we married, I got pregnant. It was very difficult for me. I felt very emotionally alone. I wanted a baby desperately. When I would go to doctor after doctor, trying to find someone who could help me conceive, I usually went alone. Sometimes Arnie would have his brother take me. His brother took me so often that the receptionist assumed he was my husband. I never explained. I was too embarrassed.

Arnie seemed happy when we found out I was finally pregnant. I was ecstatic. I remember how disappointed I was that Arnie was never available to take me to my doctor's appointments. He said he was working but I knew he was at the racetrack. I cried to his sister and she said she knew he had a problem.

Before we were married, he used to come home with Chinese food from the racetrack to make his mother think he won money. She said we were going to have this problem and told me to divorce him. I refused to listen and I never spoke to her again about the gambling until Arnie was in recovery.

He always had a new story for me and I always wanted to believe him. He'd come home very tearful and show me loan books from Household Finance and Beneficial Finance. He'd tell me, "This is what I owe and I'm never going to do this again." I wanted so much to believe that we could work our way out of that debt.

Over the years, I learned to understand the grip his gambling addiction had on him. Even when he knew he was going to lose, he had to make the bet. Arnie would play gin rummy with Marty the upstairs neighbor. Marty's wife told me my husband gambled too much. All the while, Arnie said he knew Marty was cheating him. My father told Arnie that Marty was cheating, and they were playing for big money. Now Arnie shakes his head and says, "I think I beat him once in a year, and I still kept playing."

Over the years, I learned to understand
the grip his gambling addiction had on him.
Even when he knew he was going to lose,
he had to make the bet.

There were times when Arnie was out of the house so often, day and night, that I thought he had another woman. I didn't know how to explain what was happening between us and I blamed myself. I wasn't a good enough wife, or something was wrong with me, therefore, he didn't come home when he was supposed to. Or he'd come home and abruptly leave over an argument. Arnie would come home and deliberately start a fight about something, anything, and I'd scream and yell back at him. He'd call me a bitch and just walk out of the house. The last couple of years of his active addiction, he'd call before he left work and provoke an argument. He'd say he could see I was in a bitchy mood and just not come home. He'd go right to the racetrack or the card game.

I'd sit at home the rest of the night trying to figure out what wrong thing I said or what I should have done differently. *What was it about me that caused Arnie not to want to spend more time at home?*

I did everything from changing my hair color to changing the food I made for us. I'd phone him at work and try to figure out his mood, then plan ways to either fix his mood or keep it going. I'd try to sound seductive. But he wasn't hearing any of it. Somehow it was always my fault. That was his method. Somehow he would turn everything around and blame it on me. And I believed him.

I had panic attacks, couldn't catch my breath. I'd have palpitations. Twice I went to a doctor to see if I was having a heart attack. One doctor gave me Valium. My gynecologist closed the door to his office once and asked if there was something I wanted to talk about. Was there something wrong at home? He was the nicest man and I was so close to telling him everything but I just couldn't. So I said we're having some stress over money problems. Later I learned my fallopian tubes were closed. I thought it was because of the anxiety and that was one reason I couldn't become pregnant.

My husband and I had no relationship at that point. Sex was the furthest thing from our minds, and we weren't even fighting with each other. We'd just give each other dirty looks as we walked by. I was fighting all alone—screaming, yelling, and throwing things. I put my foot through the mattress. I pulled a cabinet door off the hinges. I ripped his shirts. *I was nuts.* I was barely functioning.

I realized that other people had something I didn't have, so I stopped being around other people. I isolated. I'd walk around the house wringing my hands and crying. I got sick to the point where I wasn't leaving the house. I had suicidal thoughts. I had plans about how to do myself in. I didn't know what was happening to me.

The last six months or so before Arnie convinced himself he had to get help I stayed in the house almost all the time. If I had a pediatrician appointment, I'd almost get to the door and I'd stop and call to cancel the appointment. I couldn't make it out the door.

I used to put my infant son in his carriage on the stoop outside the garden apartment; it was a different world back then and I certainly couldn't do that now. I'd put the carriage outside so he could get fresh air, and I'd watch through the blinds to see if he was up or not. I used to make up excuses that one of us was sick so I didn't have to go to family functions.

I became a compulsive housekeeper. I always had a vacuum or a can of cleanser in my hands. That was where I had control. I could polish the stove or do the bathroom tiles with GlassWax and a toothbrush. That was my domain; that's it. That's what I turned to, compulsive cleaning.

The kids would be dressed and fed, but if my daughter wanted to play a game or read a book with me I just couldn't do it. I was obsessed. I thought, *Is he going to come home? Is he not coming home? Will there be money or won't there? Is he mad at me? Is there another woman? What did I say wrong? What did I do wrong?*

The obvious question is why didn't I walk out? Well, in the '60s not many women felt they could walk out of marriages. What could I do? My husband didn't beat me, but I was a beaten-down woman. I couldn't function. How would I support myself? I had two children to clothe, feed, and keep a roof over. I felt that either I couldn't get a job or couldn't keep a job. I wouldn't give in and go back to my parents. I didn't know if they could handle having another adult and two children living in their house.

I was obsessed. I thought, *Is he going to come home? Is he not coming home? Will there be money or won't there? Is he mad at me? Is there another woman? What did I say wrong? What did I do wrong?*

I didn't even consider leaving him because I felt totally dependent on him. The saddest thing is I had resigned myself to this way of life.

Doctors were trying to prevent my miscarriage. I was staining; they put me to bed, and for a week I didn't know where Arnie was. My husband had deserted me. Arnie's sister and mother cooked for me and took care of our two kids. Arnie says now that he doesn't remember that stuff. What he does recall is hoping I would die in the hospital so he wouldn't have to tell me how bad things were.

He left me at North Shore Hospital on Long Island. He left it up to the doctors and nurses to wait for me to miscarry. I was alone and scared to death. They didn't have a vacant room so they put me in a medicine room, and when they remembered I was there, they asked if they should get my husband. They couldn't find him. I was losing a baby and they couldn't find him! He had told his boss I was in the hospital so he wouldn't be at work. And he went to the racetrack instead.

I felt nobody cared, nobody was there, and nobody was going to take care of me. I was too hurt to be angry. The hospital staff even forgot about me until somebody happened to come to the room and saw I was hemorrhaging. That was in 1968 and it's hard for me to tell this story, even years later; they had to deliver the fetus in that room.

How could this happen to me? What had I done to deserve this?

How does anybody measure that pain? The physical pain of the miscarriage passed. But other kinds of pain hurt more and lasted longer.

What do you do when you love someone and you feel they deliberately let you down? The disappointment of broken promises, of being lied to, of feeling in your stomach that you're trapped and life is only going to get worse becomes almost unbearable.

There were times when there was so little food in our apartment I was embarrassed to have my mother come to see me and her granddaughter Stacy. I used to provoke an argument with Mom so she wouldn't stop at my house; I didn't want her to see how we lived. Maybe there was a container of milk in the refrigerator and maybe there was some cheese. There was formula for Howie, our second child, but very little of it. I'd make a can of tuna fish last for three days.

My daughter was at the toddler age when they outgrow shoes so often. I could buy them for her only on her birthday, when somebody gave her a present—if Arnie didn't get his hands on the money first.

Sometimes Arnie would threaten to leave me and I'd beg him not to go. Good or bad, I was totally dependent on him. Sometimes I'd lie on the floor and plead with him that I'd be a better wife. I felt if I did some things different, life with Arnie would get better. Whatever I did or didn't do, it got worse.

Why didn't I walk away from all the pain? That's a good question, and I suppose it's the right question. And the answers are essentially the same as those of the battered wife who doesn't leave her hell and doesn't ask for help. Many people tried to help me but I just couldn't help myself.

More than fifty years later I'm *still* Sheila and I'm *still* married to Arnie, although I don't know how our marriage survived; I'm not sure how I survived. I'm glad we're still together, though. The bond of love is strong. We've worked together and each of us can recognize now the pain of what we went through—what he inflicted on me and on himself— when his gambling addiction was so strong, and how I wanted to pay him back, to get even when each of us was beginning to go through the twelve-step program of recovery. He knows what he did and I know what I did.

PAY FOR PLAY

WE KNOW THE HOUSE *always wins* and we *always lose*. How much we lose should make us open our eyes wide. A recent study by *The Week* magazine told us the biggest market for the gambling industry is the United States. American gamblers lost a staggering $119 billion in 2013—that's $119 million with three more zeroes. That's more money than Bill Gates's $72 billion or Warren Buffett's $58 billion and nearly as much as the two of them combined. How much did *we* lose?

Most of us are all right with that. Some of it we write off to entertainment—like a day at the track, a few dollars bet to hold our attention on *Monday Night Football* and the

Super Bowl, or gin rummy with friends. We have it under control as if it were just one martini before dinner.

Gambling addiction affects around 1 percent of the population. Call them compulsive gamblers—about 600,000 of them. They lose businesses, homes, their families, and their lives. An additional 2 to 3 percent of the US population, under the spell of Powerball, state lotteries, and round-the clock Internet gambling, are identified as "problem gamblers."

It happens to the best of us. The stories are tragic and more painful than fiction. A very bright man named Eddie Condon told his story to his children and grandchildren in letters with postmarks from around the country as he kept on the move. Back in Long Beach High School in the late 1940s, Eddie was so popular that the people who knew him thought he'd end up the first Catholic President of the United States. He was an honor student and a superb athlete. His basketball coach said he was the kind of player every coach loves.

Gambling addiction affects around 1 percent of the population. Call them compulsive gamblers—about 600,000 of them. They lose businesses, homes, their families, and their lives. An additional 2 to 3 percent of the US population, under the spell of Powerball, state lotteries, and round-the clock Internet gambling, are identified as "problem gamblers."

Harvard recruited him where he won three letters in basketball and the admiration of the university. He always tried his hardest to win.

He made seven tries at gambling rehabilitation and failed them all. He moved to Las Vegas, he wrote, to "charge my batteries" and to change his luck.

It wasn't only gambling that trapped him. There was heavy drinking and perhaps a trial with other drugs, which so often beckon as evil sisters. In a letter to his son, reported in his *New York Times* obituary, Condon advised others not to bet any sport that uses a ball, but to concentrate on horses and trainer manipulation. He gambled because he didn't want to walk around lucky and not know it. He died months before the fiftieth reunion of his Harvard class: heart failure brought on by kidney and liver failure. He was seventy-one. Author Neil Amdur wrote in the *Times*: "His promise was unlimited."

His compulsion was greater. An addicted gambler can't resist the urge to gamble and to chase both losses and wins. The action itself pulls him. I've been there. I know.

When I was a teenager I bet baseball exhibition games when the best players took the day off. During one spring training, I won five exhibition games in a row and the bookmaker let me hold and feel the money. Now I understand why he let me get the sensation of winning. I was at a twelve-step meeting when a young man told everyone that he threw basketball games in high school to finance his gambling. Major college scouts lost interest in his erratic play and he wound up in Division III when he felt Division I exposure would have gotten him into the NBA.

My compulsion now is to help people like that—at least to try.

They come to me with their personal tragedies. They are ordinary people with extraordinary compulsions. Respectable people with good jobs. And some who get headlines.

Athletes may be more vulnerable than the general population when you look at the soft signs of compulsive gambling: high levels of energy, unreasonable expectations of winning, very competitive personalities, distorted optimism, and bright with high IQs. Combined, these traits help to create the perfect storm.

Sports Illustrated has estimated that 78 percent of NFL players and 60 percent of NBA players seek bankruptcy protection within the first two years after their playing days are over. US athletes aren't alone. There are enough reports about European athletes getting caught up in problems as well.

Legends of Gambling in Sports

- The greatest gambling scandal in modern sports emerged in 1951 when the basketball team of City College of New York won both the 1950 NCAA and National Invitation Tournaments—the only time it's ever been done. What was also amazing was that a few months later it was revealed that several of the best CCNY players had sold out to gamblers and were shaving points—meaning they won by fewer points than the bookmakers expected, or lost when they should have won. Then it was revealed that many of CCNY's opponents from other schools and states were also shaving points. The resulting scandal involved at least eighty-six games from 1947 to 1950. Twenty players and fourteen gamblers were convicted, with some sentenced to prison. Some former University of Kentucky star players also lost the NBA franchise they had bought. But the lessons that should have been learned would be forgotten.

- Boston College suspended thirteen football players in 1996 for gambling, including two who bet against their team. And in 1979, BC basketball player Rick Kuhn was linked to the Lucchese crime family for shaving points and served twenty-eight months in prison.

- In 1970, Chet Forte was the original director of *Monday Night Football*. He created new things in TV. He had been an All-American basketball player at Columbia University and had a dream career until his gambling addiction ended it. When I was director of the New Jersey Council on Compulsive Gambling, his lawyer brought him to me and I thought he was a beautiful guy. I took Chet into my home for almost a week and listened to his stories of ups and downs. I persuaded him to go to a twelve-step meeting. I had him listen to calls on my hotline: One guy owed a million dollars; a woman had a twenty-nine-year-old son who had gambled himself into prison; etc. By the third or fourth call, Chet had tears in his eyes.

He worked hard to help himself. He took long walks and he read. He said he tried to be a better husband and father. He'd been on the road all the time, and when he was at home he would sit in a room and watch the television to follow his bets. So he never really knew his wife and daughter.

Over the years of his recovery, he got very close to them, but felt he would never be able to pay them back. He resurrected his career as a talk-show host in San Diego, and on occasion gave his selections on the week's games until a caller argued that he of all people ought to understand the peril of what he was doing. From what I was told, he didn't do that again.

He had a history of heart problems dating to the 1980s and died at the age of sixty, but I believe he was one of those people able to shed his addiction for the last years of his life.

◆ If Chet Forte's rehab was a success, Art Schlichter's was a dismal failure—a multiple, felonious flop. He was a wonderful quarterback at Ohio State in the late '70s, and he was in the top six in Heisman Trophy balloting three times. In those years, he was also a frequent customer at Scioto Downs harness track with a known major gambler. The OSU athletic department said it didn't have enough evidence to go to the NCAA when it might have had a chance to save Schlichter's career.

Really good quarterbacks are too rare to risk losing. He was fourth pick in the 1982 NFL draft and first pick of the Baltimore Colts. By midseason, he had gambled away his entire signing bonus. In the '82–'83 college basketball season, he lost $489,000 and sought help from the league because he feared being forced by gamblers to pay his debt by throwing football games. That's about the time I became involved. I drove to South Oakes treatment center on Long Island, where Schlichter was being treated, and when I first met him, I thought, *It might be a great thing for me to be involved with a famous athlete; it might be a chance to get the attention of a lot of people about this problem.*

We spoke for a few minutes and I thought he had a chance, but then a limo took him somewhere to exercise. Most treatment centers have exercise facilities, but this was a famous athlete. *He was special.* The problem with that was that he thought so, too. He had that tremendous ego of so many compulsive gamblers. He thought he was better than anybody.

I went to see him. I think he was one of the sickest people I have ever encountered. Not only did he ruin his own career and life, he knowingly hurt other people. If I weren't so familiar with what I call the broken brains of compulsive gamblers, I might say he was just a bad guy. In 1987, he pleaded guilty in a multimillion-dollar betting operation. He was charged with thirteen felony counts of swindling people out of more than $1 million.

From 1995 to 2006, he served the equivalent of ten years in forty-four various prisons and jails for fraud, forgery, and other associated charges. His compulsion was such that he convinced his public defender to smuggle a cell phone into prison so he could place bets. In 2004, he was placed in solitary confinement for four months after he was caught gambling in prison. By the time of a 2007 interview with ESPN, he estimated that he'd stolen at least $1.5 million over the years. In 2011, Schlichter was sentenced to ten years in state prison and, while under house arrest and awaiting assignment to a state prison, he tested positive for cocaine.

A reporter who recently interviewed Schlichter brought back a message for me: "In a very sincere way, Art told me to tell you that he says 'hello' and that he is sorry for anything that ever went wrong between you two. I thought he was going to cry when I mentioned your name." Too late. I might have been able to help him if that was what he had wanted. And now I think

I've said enough about the broken mentality of one compulsive gambler.

◆ NFL stars Paul Hornung and Alex Karras were suspended for the 1963 season for betting on NFL games and associating with gamblers.

◆ I warned the NFL not to give a loan to Leonard Tose, who was part owner of the Philadelphia Eagles. Tose later told a congressional hearing on compulsive gambling that he had lost $40 to $50 million. He also lost the Eagles and his trucking business.

◆ Pete Rose, a certain Hall of Fame baseball player, was ruled permanently ineligible for induction because he bet on baseball games, including his own team. He had openly boasted how he had bet on baseball, football, and basketball. After declaring his innocence for years, ultimately he admitted he needed help.

Rose was barred from baseball for life for his gambling addiction and violation of baseball's first commandment, which is, essentially: *Thou shalt not gamble on baseball*. This commandment is Major League Rule 21: Misconduct, which forbids betting on games. A printed copy of this rule must be posted in every baseball clubhouse. It says so in the last line of the rule.

Suspicion of rigged games can be fatal. This goes back to the 1919 Black Sox Scandal, when the Cincinnati Reds (whom Rose would play for decades-after-the-fact and later manage) beat the Chicago White Sox. For a while, speculation existed over whether or not Rose actually bet on baseball and that he may have been punished for what he *might* have done. Even though he has now admitted it, many believe he should still be included in the Hall of Fame.

But Rose's punishment is valid. Players who use performance-enhancing drugs are usually suspended for a specified time frame, but Rose has not admitted much remorse or provided any evidence that he has "reconfigured his life," so there has been no offer that he might earn his way back into baseball's good graces. Perhaps that finality keeps other players from admitting to a problem and asking for help.

* There is endless speculation that Michael Jordan, the first athlete to reach a worth of a billion dollars according to *Forbes*, is a dedicated gambler. It is rumored that his year away from the NBA was to get his gambling away from the league rather than to satisfy his childhood dream of being a baseball player and to please his father, which was the official statement. Certainly, Jordan did work hard at trying out for baseball, but rumors continue.

These rumors gained credibility when he went to Atlantic City the night before a playoff game in New York, when the Knicks were a real opponent, and played high stakes baccarat far into the night. Jordan says he gambled to relax. I question whether anybody gambles "to relax." Other observers argue that he is "a competition addict" rather than a gambling addict. I think there's a very thin line between them.

After practice, where he often displayed his killer instinct, Jordan liked to shoot baskets for money—for $5 a shot or $100. He wants to win at everything and he wants to be paid off now.

One day in Monte Carlo, where the Dream Team trained before the 1992 Barcelona Olympics, then-coach Chuck Daly beat Jordan by one shot on the golf course. Daly quit while he was ahead and said, "That's it. I'll never play Michael again." Early the next morning, at the crack of dawn, Jordan called Daly's room. Getting no answer, he pounded on Daly's door. He wouldn't leave until he got his rematch. He got it, and he won by a shot.

Jordan says he gambled to relax. I question whether anybody gambles "to relax." Other observers argue that he is "a competition addict" rather than a gambling addict. I think there's a very thin line between them.

Needing to get to the casino in the middle of the playoffs, playing late into the night when he should be asleep, and even admitting in court to paying $57,000 in golf gambling debts to a convicted felon and money launderer—these clues tell me Jordan has a very big thirst to gamble.

• As much as Jordan gambled at golf, professional golfer John Daly claims he blew in excess of $55 million gambling between 1991 and 2007. He said he played blackjack for two days, leaving the table only to go to the bathroom, and loved the adrenaline rush. He claimed he would play all seven hands at the blackjack table, betting as much as $15,000 on each hand. He still plays but at lower stakes with a golf career that doesn't feed him as much money as it used to. Now it's $25-a-credit slot machines and, if he's doing well, perhaps $100-a-credit machines.

♦ Charles Barkley admitted he probably lost $10 million gambling. Why would we think he was alone? Why would we think other players who had gambling problems in college wouldn't need to feed their problem as professionals?

♦ In twelve years as an NBA star, Antoine Walker earned more than $110 million and pleaded guilty to felony bad check charges after accumulating $822,500 in gambling debts he couldn't pay.

♦ Tim Donaghy, an NBA referee, went to jail as a result of his gambling addiction. He explained how an official could affect a game's outcome better than a player. Could he be the only one?

♦ In the 1960s, Mendy Rudolph was the best-known referee in the NBA. But he used to go to the racetrack in disguise. When he died, his widow told the story of how he got a call from Las Vegas offering him money to shave points in games he was working. She recalled her husband saying, "It would be the answer to all our problems. . . . All I would have to do is look away maybe one time a game. *Maybe twice.*" Could he have been the only one who considered such a thing?

I think a major college point-shaving scandal is just around the corner and when it happens, college administrators are going to ask, "How could this happen at our school?" Because they weren't paying attention to what was going on. The NCAA had me write four articles on gambling addiction for the *NCAA News* a few years ago and I have not had a single call from an administer, coach, or athletic director.

It is time for college and professional sports to outline and implement a real program to help players who might have a gambling problem. Yet college and professional sports still do not want to deal with this. They do not want the media and public to think there is a problem.

In 1996, Horace Balmer, the NBA vice president for security, heard troubling messages from me about this problem, and also from former New York mobster Michael Franzese, who admittedly had fixed games for organized crime. Franzese said that when he talked to the NBA rookies earlier that season, he was amazed at how many confided they had gambling habits.

It is time for college and professional sports to outline and implement a real program to help players who might have a gambling problem. Yet college and professional sports still do not want to deal with this. They do not want the media and public to think there is a problem.

Franzese's story of fixing college and professional games for organized crime and compromising games by finding players with gambling habits ran in an article in the *Virginian-Pilot* newspaper on May 11, 1996. The NBA knew they had a problem on their hands when the story broke.

Who was listening when Balmer reported what he was told? Tom Shine of the Reebok shoe company, which sponsors many NBA players, said in a *GQ* magazine story that he knew an NBA player who had gambled himself into real peril. The people he lost money to were not nice guys.

In 1999, I met with Balmer and some league officials and some players and officials of the players' union. I was told, "We need to know how big the gambling problem is in the NBA."

They asked me to reserve time before the next season to address every team and player in the league. They flew Sheila in with me, and we had a second meeting where they asked us to develop a gambling questionnaire that would be given to the players to answer.

So we did what they wanted. We made up a questionnaire:

Gambling Questionnaire

1. How old were you when you placed your first bet?
2. What was the biggest "win" you ever had gambling?
3. What was the biggest "loss" you ever had gambling?
4. How often do you gamble? Circle one (every day, once a week, once a month, rarely, never)
5. Did you gamble when you were in high school?
6. Did you gamble when you attended college?
7. Has the size of your bets increased over time?
8. Have you ever gambled for longer than you had planned?
9. Does gambling give you a rush?

10. Do you often find yourself craving another gambling experience?

11. Have you ever felt remorse after time spent gambling?

12. Do you need to gamble in order to feel socially accepted by your peers?

13. Do you find yourself chasing your losses?

14. Have you ever used credit cards, markers, or bookmakers in order to gamble?

15. Have you ever needed to borrow money because of gambling?

16. Have you ever tried to stop gambling for any length of time?

17. Have you ever lied about your gambling?

18. Has gambling caused you to have problems in your personal or professional relationships?

19. Has gambling negatively affected your motivation in any area of your life?

20. Has anyone in your family had a gambling problem or any other addiction?

21. Have you ever thought that you might have a gambling problem?

22. Has anyone close to you suggested that you may have a gambling problem?

It was a beginning. I waited for the league to contact me. When I hadn't heard from the NBA, I called and asked, "When do we start?"

The talks were cancelled, and the response I got was this: "They said that the higher-ups didn't want the media to find out," and "We have players gambling on airplane trips, losing all kinds of money." They must have given the questions to the players and didn't like the answers they got. Oh well. If they can't, or *won't,* deal with the problem, that's their business. I do what I can.

Sometimes, I fear, a bad guy may strongly suggest that a player throw a bad pass late in a close game, or turn his ankle in the first quarter and limp ineffectively the rest of the game.

The whisperings about suspicious NBA scores, missed shots, and fouls at the end of the game are a constant source of speculation, but the league publicly dismisses it. The length of the season and its wear-and-tear on players always produces doubt of whether players slow up because of fatigue and injury, or whether they're doing bad business. Certainly it would hurt public confidence for the league to be openly concerned. In the early years of professional basketball and then the NBA, fixed games were considered common. Today some argue that players influential enough to control games make too much money to sell out. Still, you wonder.

Sports Betting

Dennis M. and his wife looked at and rejected forty or fifty houses until they opened the door to a Cape Cod-style with a center hallway. At the top of the stairs, Dennis could see a bathroom with a telephone on the wall. "It was like a golden halo filled the house; this was it," Dennis recalled. "I could grab all my betting papers, lock the door, and make my bets." Dennis has been in a twelve-step program for more than ten years and still jumps when his daughter flips channels and pauses at a game.

He can't let himself watch the Giants or the Jets—New York City's NFL franchises. Worse yet, he had to explain to his son, who once blocked for former Giants fullback Ron Dayne in high school, that father and son couldn't go to a game together. He lamented, "We were both cheated out of one of the joys of life."

When you open the sports pages, the betting lines are advertised as if they were the best buys in the supermarket. ESPN, the TV sports station, televises poker competitions so you can see if you're as slick as the players on screen. Harrah's casinos advertise at Citi Field, the Mets' home of the family game. The National Collegiate Athletic Association (NCAA), which governs the games, and the professional leagues should have enough clout to stop this if they wanted to. The NCAA has talked about refusing credentials to newspapers and stations who run the lines, but that hasn't happened yet.

On a TV show a few years ago, retired basketball coach and noted sports moralist Bobby Knight grumbled that a newspaper publishing point spreads should also publish addresses of prostitutes and drug peddlers.

And when gamblers want action, it's only as far away as televised college games, even between schools they may never have heard of, or *Monday Night Football*, which gives them a chance to get even after their weekend losses. Lots of viewers mean lots of money.

Former NBA commissioner David Stern said, "We don't want the week's grocery money to be bet on the outcome of a particular sporting event." Yet, in 2009, he told *Sports Illustrated* that legalized gambling on the NBA "may be a huge opportunity." I wonder how many addicted gamblers placed their first bet on an NBA game.

In 2014, the New Jersey Supreme Court rejected a proposal to have legalized betting on sports events. That pleased me. Now to bet on a ball game, New Jerseyites have to travel to Las Vegas or look for a bookmaker like I did.

The histories presented in this chapter are a sad reminder, a snapshot, of just how bad it can get. But these stories are about *adults* who got in trouble with the bet. Many of these gamblers didn't start down that road late in life. Sadly, many began as children or young adults and already had a history—many before they were old enough to drink.

The most challenging problem on the college campus isn't drinking or drugs but uncontrolled gambling. Odds and point spreads are cafeteria conversation: "There goes tuition and room and board. Who will loan me $500?"

I'll talk about young gamblers in the next chapter because the early signs of a problem are often missed.

The most challenging problem on the college campus isn't drinking or drugs but uncontrolled gambling.

5 ♣

ON THE BRINK

YOUNG PEOPLE ARE GETTING in trouble earlier and the symptoms of their gambling go unnoticed for too long. And some of these young people are smart and are able to hide their gambling from others. Many parents have their kids program their DVD players or fix their computers because they can't figure out how. Kids are too smart for their own good.

The signs are there if you know what to look for. I discuss the signs of a gambling problem in more detail in the next chapter. First, in this one, I offer some statistics:

- Based on the results of fourteen studies of people with gambling problems, young people suffer from disordered gambling at about two to three times the rates of adults.

- A Canadian survey of 1,471 college students found that nearly 27 percent of the pathological gamblers among them didn't just fantasize about killing themselves, but had actually attempted suicide. That's a scary statistic!

- Of the calls to my gambling hotline (1-888-LAST-BET) in the last five years, one third were from young poker players between the ages of twelve and thirty or from parents of these young people.

I've come to know that there are so many young people in trouble or on the brink, and they need help.

I see kids all the time who don't want to go to college; they want to be professional poker players. I hear from both high school and college students about how they struggle with the bet. Here are some common gambling behaviors taken from their stories:

- Paying someone else to take exams or write papers so as not to interfere with time needed to gamble.

- Betting on games they were playing in.

- Gambling underage in legal gambling establishments.

- Shaving points in high school while being looked at by Division I colleges.

- Robbing a convenience store and a bank for money with which to gamble.

- Using fake credit cards, bouncing checks, and creating phony checking accounts to get money for gambling.

- Selling drugs and their bodies to pay gambling debts.

- Stealing objects and money from other students, or from college property.

- Selling or pawning property that belonged to the college they were attending.

- Running bookmaking rings, football pools, or card games in college in order to pay off gambling debts.

- Using tuition money for gambling.

- Using financial aid or other loans for gambling.

- Conning their parents into sending additional money, which is later used for gambling.

- Stealing cars, items, or money from employers for gambling.

- Selling personal property for gambling money.

One young gambler's story, in particular, has had a lasting impression on me. He was from Mississippi and lived in our home for four weeks trying to start his recovery from gambling addiction. This young man played college football and even appeared in a bowl game. He was also a track star for his college. His gambling started with a $5 football pool card and progressed to the point of embezzling $350,000 from his employer.

College administrators know that gambling is a greater danger among students than binge drinking. Tuitions are lost. Odds and point spreads are normal conversation. Gambling is more available than beer or cigarettes. The student bookmakers get their betting lines straight out of the local newspapers. Sometimes the magnetism pulls in a college athlete who is in a position to influence the outcome of a game and can place a bet on that game. He draws his own conclusions.

The Seeds Are Being Planted

When I was with the New Jersey Council on Compulsive Gambling, we'd have workshops on children's issues and how they become addicted. I saw kids having poker parties at home. Kids told me their first gambling experience was when mother and father took them to a casino. They had to stay behind a line on the casino carpet, but they could watch the adults at the tables all excited and having a good old time. Parents buy scratch-off tickets and win five dollars, and the child at their side thinks it's "free money." That's a growing issue in our twelve-step programs: young people's proximity to gambling. It plants the seed.

But there is little demand for treatment for kids playing poker in elementary school. A teacher told me she walked into her seventh-grade classroom during lunchtime and found kids shooting craps in the back of the room—*seventh-graders*, probably twelve years old. She sent them to the principal's office; the principal said, "What do you want me to do?" I guarantee if they had been drinking alcohol, he'd have called their parents.

One principal came to me and told me he had two pupils with gambling problems and I found a twelve-step program for them. I know of Long Island kids only fourteen years old, and lots of other young people under twenty-one years old, with problems that were allowed to get worse. It never used to be like that.

I guarantee if they had been drinking alcohol, he'd have called their parents.

Children of Gamblers

I had finished a talk at a treatment center in New Jersey when a woman came to me and nervously asked to speak to me privately. She said she was fifty-four years old and never understood that her father was addicted to gambling until she heard what I'd said.

"I lived in Ohio and my dad was a gambler," she said. "As a teen my dad would take me to his bookmaker to sleep with him to pay off his gambling losses. I did that through all of my teen years. Today I am an alcoholic and have been in recovery for ten years."

She asked to speak to the group of people in treatment and she blew them away. Her story left them—and me— in tears.

It was a stunning moment for me, and telling her story must have been excruciating for her. I don't know whether telling me was part of her addiction treatment, or if I was the first person she told. What she had to endure was horrific, but it opened my mind to the realization that in our effort to help compulsive gamblers, we pay hardly any attention to young people caught up in the addiction of others, and who are likely to develop their own. And yet, when these kids grow up, they carry with them the memories of what it was like living in the destruction created by parents who were compulsive gamblers.

I have a friend who told me that his parents gambled on horses, sports, or in casinos. They always seemed to be short of money when he needed something, but they had money to wager. I have another friend whose father lost millions and millions of dollars and then stole $150,000 from him, but who also grew up to be a compulsive gambler and is now in recovery.

Many kids of compulsive gamblers are great successes later in life. I read the story of Barbara Walters, a remarkably successful woman. Her father, Lou, was a businessman and compulsive gambler. He made and then lost fortunes and was never home. I also read about Bob Costas's father, who bet on ballgames. More and more stories are coming out from these kids, now adults, whose childhoods included a parent with a gambling habit.

Many adults carry around the baggage of less-than-perfect childhoods. But some outgrow it, some thrive, and some, like Barbara Walters and Bob Costas, seem to overcome it and succeed despite their challenges. Others, sadly, like my friend whose father stole from him, also wind up compulsive gamblers. You just never know.

When There's Compulsive Gambling in the Family

There are many professionals who believe that addictive tendencies are inherited. A recent study published in the *Journal of Clinical Psychiatry* found that family members of compulsive gamblers are eight times more likely to develop pathological gambling in their lifetime than other people. That's a higher rate than with many other psychiatric disorders.

Those people who know they have a gambling problem should be especially aware of what's going on with their children. You know, the apple doesn't fall far from the tree. Tell your kids they share your genes and what that means to them. They should recognize their own warning signs and know that help is available. They need to be aware of themselves and understand that many children of gamblers often become addicted, too.

A recent study published in the *Journal of Clinical Psychiatry* found that family members of compulsive gamblers are eight times more likely to develop pathological gambling in their lifetime than other people. That's a higher rate than with many other psychiatric disorders.

Sheila and I believe it's important to be honest and to let your children know about your addiction. Kids watch sports on TV, and they are drawn to the big events of the Super Bowl in professional football and the Final Four in college basketball; gatherings of family and friends are built around big sporting events, which is healthy for most of them. We encourage them to go outside and play the games—from Little League to recreation league softball. But then we can't tell them that we can't watch the big game with them because it's dangerous for us?

A friend of mine is a professional man who has been in our program for twenty years and has a thirteen-year-old son who wanted to celebrate his bar mitzvah with a poker party. Dad couldn't do that. He has two other children, sixteen and nineteen years old, and I told him to tell them all what's going on with his life. The kids would see their mother and father go out one evening every week and never say where. When the father finally did tell the kids that he was a compulsive gambler and had been going to twelve-step gambling meetings, the nineteen-year-old asked his father: "What else did you lie to us about all these years?" It might have been a lot easier to tell them a long time ago.

Compulsive gambling doesn't discriminate. It happens in the best of families. And how do they get out of it? Usually by way of a crisis, or a friend or family member notices that something is wrong. My hope is for these people to get help before they wind up in a jail or an institution, or worse. Young people may lack the proper coping skills, and older gamblers feel isolated, alone, and that nobody understands. Well, I understand, and I try to help them.

Help for Gambling-Addicted Youth

In our twelve-step programs, we don't reach young people well enough. We in the fellowship haven't fully absorbed the fact that gambling has become so socially acceptable in our society. Way back when, there were twelve-step programs for gamblers in fewer than twelve states. When I was young, gambling was legal only in Las Vegas, Reno, and the racetracks, which had minimum ages. So most younger people had to play poker at home, or find a way to bet on sports events with a bookmaker. It wasn't as easy to find action.

Few twelve-step programs deal with young people in trouble with gambling, but more are starting to do so. Still, the kids usually reject those forty- and fifty-year-olds, their advice, and the very notion that one day they could be in the same predicament as those "old folks." Kids come to our meetings and see fifty-year-olds and say, "I'd never be like that. I never stole anything." *Uh-huh*, I may think or even say under my breath—*yet*.

I helped start a youth meeting in New Jersey; two of those kids came back eighteen or twenty years later with gambling problems. Of course, countless unidentified young people are at the same stage where we were—some strong enough to control their urges, and a few terribly vulnerable.

We are seeing so many more young people coming for help. Most of them are poker players who believe they can be poker champions and that it will make them rich—so no need for them to go to school anymore. I think a third of our hotline calls are from parents of kids hooked on gambling or from the kids themselves, some of them as young as twelve years old.

Sheila ran a twelve-step program for young people in New Jersey, and next she tells the story of her involvement with it.

SHEILA'S EXPERIENCE

I wish more people remembered that youth program. The concept was to get kids to understand that their parents' gambling problem wasn't their fault. Many kids believe that if only they did better in school, their parents wouldn't argue so much. They're often resentful of the non-gambling parent for demanding that the gambling parent have more self-control. Kids who live in a home with money and a high-rolling parent who is welcome at the casinos and fancy hotels can get hooked on that lifestyle.

In our society, gambling is still widely accepted; it's not seen as a danger. Parents who do recognize the problem would like to talk about it and share their awareness of the danger.

Some kids think that gambling makes you rich. I tell parents to watch for a fascination with seeking the big win. Watch the kid whose friends like to play poker and notice if yours is watching gambling on TV. A lot of kids are involved in poker, not drugs, for the big high.

Too many parents feel that gambling is no big deal, so these early indications can be eye-openers. In addition:

Observe the personality traits for grandiose thinking: Does he or she boast and brag?

Listen for unrealistic optimism: "Somebody wins; why not me?"

And watch for the mentality that says problem gambling only happens to somebody else.

In some communities, the Parent-Teacher Association (PTA) will discuss the issue, but some of the parents involved think that addressing childhood gambling is an intrusion into their lives. In our society, gambling is still widely accepted; it's not seen as a danger. Parents who *do* recognize the problem would like to talk about it and share their awareness of the danger.

If all the kids are gambling, it's hard for one to just stay away. Peer pressure is rough. The need for acceptance and inclusion will drive children and teens to the brink. Nobody knows who is going to go on to develop full-blown addiction, but somebody will.

Maybe the spelling tests should include 1-888-LAST-BET.

TEMPTATIONS AND TIP-OFFS
TO TROUBLE

IT LOOKS LIKE GOOD, clean, innocent fun, like a beer on the beach or a boy's night out. Addiction is usually hidden until gamblers become unable to stop. They begin to exclude other activities from their social lives. Companions become limited to other gamblers. Life becomes a search for money to gamble. So much of life becomes a lie. After they hit a real bottom, perhaps they'll wind up in prison like former college and professional football player and compulsive gambler Art Schlichter did.

Maybe this all sounds like exaggeration in the way the film *Reefer Madness*—a 1936 film classic about the evils of marijuana—was laughed at until it had no value. But we find gamblers are drawn to their bets like drug addicts needing a fix. I say they have broken brains. Even if they want to escape, they won't know how. They'll try and fail again and again.

Temptation is Everywhere

If I were gambling today, I would end up in jail. There are so many more easy temptations now than when I became addicted.

When I finally stopped in 1968, only three states had a lottery. The Super Bowl was just developing its magnet for the bettor. There was no *Monday Night Football*. The big horse tracks in the east closed for the winter months. There were no phones in the racetracks and no telephone betting. There was no off-track betting and no legal betting on credit, and illegal betting on credit was at the whim of the kindly bookmaker. ATMs were not around yet. There were no bus trips to gambling dens and no Internet gambling, either. Riverboat gambling was only on the Mississippi.

Fortunately for me, credit cards were very uncommon at the time or I would have abused them so badly that no twelve-step program could have helped me make a repayment budget.

Today, the Super Bowl draws more than $100 million legally for Las Vegas and unknown millions for bookmakers. College football and Sunday professional games encourage greater gambling than ever, and the weeknight NFL game—when Saturday and Sunday losers feel they can get even or make up their losses—draws more betting than the weekend matches.

A classic example of all this involves the National Football League and how we used to bet which team won and lost the game and by how many points. Some of the exotic bets now are almost a laughing matter, they're so extreme. With the Super Bowl played in February, you could bet over-and-under on the total scoring or on the temperature at kickoff—over/under by thirty-two degrees. Or you could bet what the first score of a game would be. Who'd have thought the first score in a Super Bowl would have been a two-point safety? But it happened, and I am sure somebody bet it. Of course, you could bet heads or tails on the pregame coin toss, as happened to the guy who lost $22,000 on that in the Giants' Super Bowl win years ago.

It was estimated that $10 million was bet on the 2014 Super Bowl game, legally or illegally. *How many people won and how many lost*, I wonder.

And if we don't bet football, there are so many other sporting events beckoning. College games are on TV day and night.

Harness racing has faded from popularity, and thoroughbred racing, once called "the sport of kings," has declined steeply except for its three springtime jewels—the Kentucky Derby, the Preakness Stakes, and the Belmont Stakes. Think of the continuous promotion of California Chrome, winner of the 2014 Kentucky Derby and the Preakness, coming to the Belmont on the first Saturday in June with a chance to be the first horse in four decades to win the Triple Crown.

It was a story full of the romance of racing. The stories were in your eyes and ears and face, and 102,000 people were drawn to Belmont Park for the race. I hadn't watched the Kentucky Derby for years and years. Racing fed my growing addiction when I was a kid, but you can't escape what's going on around you—not just on the sports programs, but in the daily news. That's stressful to someone in recovery. I was in the car when the Belmont post positions were announced and radio sports commentator Mad Dog explained that California Chrome had won the Preakness from post position two and had the same post position for the Belmont.

Wow, gamblers are superstitious! If I won a bet after using a particular bathroom, I'd go back to that same bathroom before betting the next race. So hearing a "two" and "two" on post positions could seem like a good sign. But you may remember that California Chrome finished fourth in the Belmont; anyone enticed by the post positions lost their bet. Those big events don't affect me now, but I'm sure they jiggled my innards early on.

And yet you have to know what you shouldn't be doing. I still can't go to a racetrack. I turn off the nightly news if they're about to show the finish of the day's feature race. If I so much as drive past the former site of Roosevelt Raceway on Long Island, I feel a tug, even though where the old place used to be is now a shopping mall.

Racing is called a sport, but if there were no betting, who would go? Now TV is calling poker a sport. Televised poker competitions are as good to watch as game shows. There is live racing and exotic poker on TV, so no one has to miss out on the action.

In fact, you can hardly browse the Internet or watch the sports channels without coming across some kind of poker tournament or a pop-up ad about poker or an e-mail inviting you to come play and have a good time—*and maybe hit the jackpot.*

Lottery is all over the land, from those promising payoffs in hundreds of millions to scratch-offs in the candy store next to the school bus stop. After all, they say, "You have to be in it to win it."

The lottery in its many forms is a subtle, apparently innocent gateway, as some people call it; like marijuana is a gateway drug. What's the danger in giving twenty-one scratch-off cards for a twenty-first birthday? Well, what's the danger in a can of beer for a fourteen-year-old after a softball game? It's a piece of paper to scratch and maybe a win of two dollars. But for a few, it's a spark that kindles a fire. The big-money Irish Sweepstakes ended in 1987, but because state lotteries are all across America now, nobody has to wait anymore to win a million bucks. Besides, lottery money goes to education, doesn't it? That is, what's left—after executive salaries and sellers' fees, advertising, and other expenses—goes to education.

Ironically, many college administrators whose schools receive lottery funding now say gambling is a bigger problem for students than drugs and alcohol; tuitions are lost in fraternity house and dormitory poker games.

Women gamblers are the new target. Women historically like to play the slots, and the lure of slot machines has attracted more women than ever, but they've also been edging up toward the big time. At least half of my calls for help come from women. My colleague Dave S., who used to work with a twelve-step program on Long Island, watched women put their children on the school bus in the morning and play scratch-off cards and Quick Draw at Mel's Stationery until the kids came home. There are no warning symptoms there, are there?

And so it goes.

Easy Access and Lenders

There are so many opportunities to place a bet and get money to place one that didn't exist before I quit in 1968.

It's one thing to place a bet with money you have, but today you can place one with money you *don't* have. By the time problem gamblers are recognized these days, they have lost staggering amounts of their money, their family's money, the credit card company's money, and the payday loan company's money. Thank god I didn't have credit cards. Today's lenders must know what the deal is, but they don't cut off the money for the many gamblers who have credit accounts. They keep lending more. *That's a problem.*

ATMs weren't everywhere like they are today—including at casinos and racetracks. Checks are even accepted at casinos. I didn't have access to equity loans or markers to finance my gambling. Back in those days, my bookie placed the bets and on Mondays I would settle up with him. If I didn't have the money, he might not take my next bet.

Some states have three lottery picks a day, and huge payoffs on Powerball promise unimaginable wealth. When the lottery was new, cashiers sold the tickets and looked to see if you were eighteen years old. Now they have stand-alone machines that sell tickets and the cashier doesn't even see who's buying them. Scratch-off lottery tickets are so commonly available, it makes it hard for a recovering gambler to buy gas or get a quart of milk in a convenience store without having to fight the lure.

Today, we also have electronic betting in many bars, plus Internet gambling at home, so you don't even have to leave your house; you can gamble in your underwear. Six states have legalized telephone gambling and everyone has a cell phone.

And, of course, casinos are popping up everywhere. There are casinos in more than thirty states, with 80 percent of Americans living within 200 miles of a gambling establishment.

Back in the '60s, casinos in New Jersey opened at 10:00 a.m. and closed at 4:00 a.m. In 1980, casinos in New Jersey wanted to start twenty-four-hour gambling. I didn't support that and got calls from the industry trying to convince me not to talk to the media about how bad an idea it was.

Today, casinos are open twenty-four hours a day in many parts of the country. And slot machines are popping up in places other than casinos. You don't have to go to Las Vegas or Atlantic City anymore to place a bet. You can stay close to home to do that.

Casinos also advertise in ballparks all over the country. They operate restaurants and bars at Yankee Stadium and Citi Field in New York and in several other ballparks, but what they really do under the cloak of sports is advertise for casino gambling.

We wouldn't expect to open the newspaper and get a price list of illegal drugs for sale or a listing where the hookers are working. But that's just about what we can get when we open the sports pages of newspapers all over the country. You don't see drug prices, but you do see betting lines and point spreads on sports events.

Betting lines and ads for gambling information are viral. Gambling talk is all over radio and television. There are opportunities being advertised in the media for gambling full-time, all the time.

We wouldn't expect to open the newspaper and get a price list of illegal drugs for sale or a listing of where the hookers are working. But that's just about what we can get when we open the sports pages of newspapers all over the country. You don't see drug prices, but you do see betting lines and point spreads on sports events. It used to be that you couldn't place a legal bet on sports anywhere in America except in Las Vegas, but now we are surrounded by legal and illegal betting that's readily available.

There are also newspapers ads for 800 and 900 phone numbers that sell information to gamblers. Some of these ads shout, "Get the game of the month free," "We pick 75 percent winners," "Last week we went eleven for twelve," and "Get our lock of the week."

And don't miss the chance to get rich quick. I remember when *The Dallas Morning News* had a gorilla in the zoo making football picks for them. The gorilla's picks were doing better than the so-called experts'.

The media report the problem of compulsive gambling while at the same time advertising their point-spreads and betting advice free-of-charge. They do not include advisories that people with problems should call 1-888-LAST-BET. Hypocrisy is free.

Of course, not everyone gets caught up and drawn over the line. Some will watch or participate a bit and then move on. Some will be hooked. The game of poker is quick and can be fun, full of table talk and laughter, sometimes with sandwiches and coffee. People have been playing that way for a long time, and it's a good time. But *that* kind of gambling also fits comfortably with someone who has an impulse disorder, which is what compulsive gambling is. It can be a magnetic and dangerous attraction for a developing or recovering compulsive gambler.

How to Tell If You (or Someone You Love) Has a Problem with Gambling

Before you can deal with the problem, first you have to recognize what a compulsive gambler is. Then look at yourself in the mirror. At some point, you will have to be honest with yourself about whether you match the profile, and it may take a while.

I still didn't believe after I made my last bet that I was a compulsive gambler. I still had the idea I was going to win a lot of money. *Then I could be satisfied and I'd quit on my own*, I thought. I was positive I could quit. You know who stops on their own? People who aren't addicted. If you see someone in the mirror whose life is unmanageable, someone thinking of embezzling at work, ashamed of stealing from the kids' piggy bank, or not paying bills, give yourself this test:

The American Psychiatric Association (APA) defines the compulsive gambler as someone with recurrent and persistent behavior, as evidenced by at least five of the following signs (most people who aren't problem gamblers would have to strain to identify three):

1. Preoccupied with gambling: Preoccupied with reliving past gambling experiences, planning or handicapping the next venture, or thinking of ways to get or find more money with which to gamble.

2. Needs to gamble with increasing or larger amounts of money in order to achieve desired excitement.

3. Repeated and unsuccessful efforts to stop, cut back, or control their gambling.

4. Irritable or restless when attempting to stop or cut down on their gambling.

5. Gambles to escape from life problems or relieve a mood, such as feelings of anxiety, helplessness, guilt, or depression.

6. After losing money while gambling, often returns to get even ("chasing" losses).

7. Lies to therapist, family members, friends, or others to conceal the full extent of his or her gambling.

8. Has committed illegal acts, such as forgery, theft, fraud, or embezzlement, to finance gambling.

9. Has lost or jeopardized a job, significant relationship, educational, or other career opportunity because of gambling.

10. Relies on other people to provide money to relieve a worsening or desperate financial situation caused by gambling.

The American Medical Association (AMA) suggests physicians advise patients of the addictive potential of gambling, as shown in the following chart.

GAMBLING DISORDER AND RECOVERY CHART

WINNING PHASE

Occasional gambling
Excitement
Fantasies about winning
Increased amounts bet
Big win

LOSING PHASE

Can't stop gambling
Preoccupied with gambling
Losing time from work
Personality changes
Heavy borrowing
Careless about spouse/family
Covering up/lying
Bailouts

DESPERATION PHASE

Alienation from
family and friends
Marked increase in amount
and time spent gambling
Illegal acts
Panic
Remorse

HOPELESSNESS PHASE

Suicidal thoughts and attempts
Arrests
Divorce
Alcohol

CRITICAL PHASE

Responsible thinking
Decision-making
Hopeful
Realistic; stops gambling
Honest desire for help

REBUILDING PHASE

Develop goals
Self-respect returning
Improving spouse and
family relationships
New interests
Budget/paying bills

GROWTH PHASE

New way of life
Facing problems promptly
Giving affection to others
Preoccupation with
gambling decreases
Insight into self

Spotting Gambling Addiction in a Spouse

Sheila is the expert on recognizing and unraveling deception in a problem gambler. I'll let her explain what she learned.

SHEILA'S EXPERIENCE

What living with Arnie taught me is that when people get hints of a problem they look the other way. I also learned that if your gut tells you something might be wrong, chances are you're right.

The tip-offs that someone you know is a compulsive gambler include unexplained money issues: something not being paid on time when you were told it was; bank statements with large withdrawals; suspicious and mysterious phone calls with whispered conversation. Also watch out for your spouse isolating him- or herself and being focused on some solitary activity.

Sometimes gambling addiction is so hidden that you don't know about it. I would say, "That can't be," or ask Arnie to calm me down. I'd check if the stock was still there, if I was coming out of the fog enough to pursue the answers. The evidence may be in a credit report that reveals the credit cards are maxed out, an equity loan was secretly taken out, or there's a second mortgage that you weren't told about.

You need to be vigilant about your own finances; some spouses never look at their own checkbook. If the hint is obvious enough, don't go to the gambler for the answer; have someone else examine what you saw. Part of the gambler's manipulation is convincing you that there's no need for you to know what's going on.

My generation was taught that the husband takes care of finances, and it's hard to go against what a trusting, loving relationship should be. But if there's an addiction, the rules have to change. Consult a lawyer or a tax attorney. Gamblers forge signatures. Countless times I thought we had paid off a loan, and at the end of the month I'd find it had been renegotiated and had never been paid off. I used to call Arnie with questions and he was always ready with a false explanation.

You can also consult the International Service Office of Gam-Anon, the twelve-step program for families of compulsive gamblers. Visit their website at Gam-Anon.org or call them at 718-352-1671. They can provide literature with more information on how to recognize gambling addiction and what to do or not do if you think there is a problem. You could almost say they will hold your hand. Be strong.

The Importance of Identifying Compulsive Gambling in Young People

One-third of the calls to the 1-888-LAST-BET helpline in recent years have come from young people between fifteen and thirty years old or from their parents. In Chapter Five, I explained many of the problems these young gamblers have already experienced. With the age of Internet gambling and televising of gambling as if it were another sports event, we expect the average age of people looking for help will drop and more of those identified with a gambling problem will be younger.

We know from years of experience that the younger a person is or the earlier in somebody's life gambling becomes a habit, the more likely it is to become a compulsion. The other side of the coin is that the earlier treatment begins, the more effective it is.

A survey of adult male recovering gamblers showed that 96 percent began gambling before the age of fourteen. By age fourteen, I was already into playing pinball machines and betting the stock market. Because compulsive gambling is so much more manageable and treatable in its early stages, I believe that if I had recognized my own problem and found help when I was a kid, I could have saved Sheila and myself so much heartache.

Sheila and I have prepared some questions for parents that may help determine whether their kids have a gambling problem.

Questions for Young People and Parents

1. Do you find yourself gambling more frequently than you used to?

2. Has anyone ever suggested that you have a problem with gambling?

3. Did you ever gamble more than you intended to? (Either time-wise or money-wise)

4. Do you have a fantasy that gambling is going to make you rich?

5. Do you believe you have superior knowledge when you place a bet?

6. Do you lose time from school due to gambling?

7. Do you have intense interest in point spreads or odds?

8. Do you make frequent calls to sports phones or lotteries?

9. Have you ever bet with a bookmaker and signed a marker or used credit cards to gamble?

10. Have your grades dropped because of gambling?

11. Have you ever done anything illegal to finance your gambling?

12. Are gambling language or references part of your vocabulary?

13. Do you prefer to socialize with friends who gamble?

14. Does anyone in your family have an addiction?

15. Have you ever borrowed money to finance gambling?

16. Has anyone ever bailed you out and paid your gambling debts for you?

17. Does gambling give you a "rush" or "high"?

18. Do you find yourself craving another gambling experience?

19. Do you find yourself "chasing" your losses or wins?

20. Have you ever tried to stop or control your gambling?

21. Have you lied about your gambling to family and/or friends?

22. Are you spending more time on the Internet?

23. Are you playing poker, betting sports, or playing casino games on the Internet?

If you are a parent, ask if these conditions apply to your son or daughter. If you conclude there are too many "yes" answers, call the hotline at 1-888-LAST-BET or e-mail me at ASWexler@aol.com.

Casino Exclusion Lists

Some casinos let people bar themselves by putting their names on an exclusion list, but to do that people are required to attest they have a gambling problem. Several states have exclusion laws enabling gamblers to enlist for one year, five years, or their lifetime. And casinos do have self-interest, and will sometimes exclude people who don't pay their debts.

It's my experience that voluntary exclusion doesn't work, as much as the gambler may think it will. There are as many holes in the process as in Swiss cheese. Eventually the exclusion period expires and then it's back to the tables or the slots or the sports book. Even if it does work for a few people at casinos, there are so many other places and ways to gamble.

I believe it's foolish for addicted gamblers to think that down the road they will be able to gamble and be in control. It's also mindless for a casino to admit someone who once had a gambling problem, especially when they can be sued for permitting entrance to a person known to be a compulsive gambler.

Voluntary exclusion sounded like a good idea at the time it was created, but we have learned a lot since then. A well-intentioned gambler may put himself or herself on exclusion in New Jersey, and in a few days drive to a casino in Pennsylvania instead. I've talked to countless addicted gamblers who've gone back to gambling after being excluded and find themselves worse off than before. I go to twelve-step recovery meetings often and I hear people say, "I'm on the exclusion list, but I keep going to gamble; I can't stop myself."

Recovery works one day at a time.
It is a process.

I find that self-exclusion is really self-deception. A small group of addicted gamblers may seek and find real help, but the key is to get into a real recovery program, not just stay out of the casinos. Recovery works one day at a time. It is a process.

ARNIE'S LIFE IN ACTIVE ADDICTION VS LIFE IN RECOVERY	
ACTIVE ADDICTION	LIFE IN RECOVERY
Wished to die every day.	Can't wait to face each new day.
Thought only of myself.	Wake up every day thinking of others.
Phone bill made me angry.	Today, I am a lot less angry.
Unable to talk about feelings for weeks.	Can openly show and talk about feelings today.
When kids talked, I never heard them.	Listen to children today, hearing what they say.
When Sheila talked, I never heard a word she said.	Listen to Sheila today; I hear her and ask questions.
Stole something every day.	Haven't stolen anything in years.

| ARNIE'S LIFE IN ACTIVE ADDICTION VS LIFE IN RECOVERY ||
ACTIVE ADDICTION	LIFE IN RECOVERY
Said "yes" to everything.	Don't just say "yes" when I really want to say "no."
Unable to express feelings in writing.	Able to express feelings in writing.
Lied about everything and couldn't stop lying.	Today, I don't lie and haven't lied for years.
Unable to say "I love you."	Tell people all the time that I love them.
Unable to say "I am sorry."	Today, if I do something I wish I didn't do, I can say "I am sorry" and truly mean it.
Always hurt everyone's feelings.	I think before I speak and am considerate of other's feelings.
Stuffed my feelings.	Able to openly show and discuss feelings.
Didn't care about myself.	Today, I care about myself.
Lived with emotional hurt and pain.	Love my life today.
Cried myself to sleep at night.	Able to sleep well at night.
Every night I came home, I swore off gambling.	Last bet was April 10, 1968.
Felt the pain of gambling 24/7.	Experience peace and calm.
Constantly searching for gambling money.	Financially secure and stable today.
Lacked coping skills.	Today, I have coping skills.
"Bumps in the road of life" were an excuse to go on a gambling spree.	"Bumps in the road of life" are opportunities for me to grow and learn; I take them in stride.
Thought about gambling day and night.	Today, I have a clear head and am not obsessed with gambling.
Had no one to talk to or confide in.	I have a twelve-step program, sponsor, and wife to talk to and confide in.
Thought my only answer to money problems was a big win.	Today, I live within my means and have a budget.

ARNIE'S LIFE IN ACTIVE ADDICTION VS LIFE IN RECOVERY	
ACTIVE ADDICTION	**LIFE IN RECOVERY**
Thought suicide was the only way out of misery.	Today, I don't even consider it.
I knew the next bet would be the big win.	Today, I know gambling isn't the answer.
Prayed to God for winning bets.	Today, I pray for my recovery.
Bet money I had and money I didn't have.	Today, I value my life and my money.
Couldn't hug my wife and kids.	I hug my wife and kids everyday.
Used to only have "gambling buddies."	Today, I have many true friends.
Trusted no one.	Today, I trust many people.
Had no hope I could stop gambling.	In recovery a long time (forty-six years).

7

TWELVE-STEP RECOVERY FOR COMPULSIVE GAMBLERS AND THEIR FAMILIES

TWELVE-STEP PROGRAMS ARE FUNDAMENTALLY based on ancient spiritual principles and rooted in sound medical therapy. The best recommendation for these programs is the fact that they work. But compulsive gamblers are complicated people. They over think things. They want to know *how* they work; they try to figure them out. It doesn't matter how or why they work—I don't know how electricity works, but I use it—only that they do for some people.

I was skeptical that the twelve-step program was going to work for me. I wasn't even sure I *wanted* the program to work for me. And I wasn't sure I *wanted* to stop gambling. I was going to twelve-step meetings and I didn't want to be there. I had the notion that they would give me the money I needed. I heard the things people stood up and said about quitting gambling and I thought they were lying. I'm sure I was one of any number of doubters.

My recollection of those first days is greatly colored by the fact that the program worked for me and I've been free of the weight of gambling all these years. I'm pretty damn proud of that. I don't remember just why I kept attending meetings, other than that Sheila was urging me to go. She also joined the program for family members of gamblers, and she believed in twelve-step recovery much more than I did. I have to give her so much credit for how it worked for me. She'll tell her side of the story later in this chapter.

Sheila and I put our heads together and came up with a list of common myths that gamblers tell themselves. The myths come from their delusional thinking and are a big obstacle to getting help. Until they get it through their heads that these myths and their gambling are killing them, they can't really embrace recovery.

Nine Gambling Myths

1. The big win is just around the corner with the next bet I make.

2. I can get even again; *then* I will stop gambling.

3. I am not like drug addicts or alcoholics.

4. I can stop any time I want; I just don't want to stop.

5. I am too young to be a gambling addict.

6. If I had more money, I know I could win.

7. I am smarter than the rest of the gamblers.

8. The losses are not my fault right now; I'm just having bad luck.

9. I know I can beat this game.

These myths and many others keep gamblers out there chasing their wins and their losses. Usually, the gambler will have a personal crisis that will get him or her into recovery. Recovery isn't easy, but it is possible. Many gamblers find their way to a twelve-step recovery program.

The twelve-step fellowship of recovery intends to highlight that compulsive gambling is an illness, and to provide an alternative to the destruction it causes in our lives. Our ranks are filled with members who have recovered from the illness by stopping gambling and attaining a normal way of life, and these members remain ready to help any other individual who passes through our door.

What Your First Twelve-Step Meeting Will Be Like

At your first meeting, the leader will announce there is a new person in the room. The group will cheer, and then members will share about things that went on in their lives that explain why they're at the meeting. The objective is to make everyone—especially newcomers—understand that they are not alone. Somebody will read "The Twenty Questions," the checklist of compulsive gambling signs, out loud. They will ask you what you want out of being there.

>The objective is to make everyone—
>especially newcomers—understand
>that they are not alone.

In your mind, you may ask, *Who is in charge and why?* The meeting leader is someone the group elects, usually for a six-month period, who is a fellow recovering gambler, not a doctor or therapist without a history of compulsive gambling themselves. Sometimes the group will select another leader for just one night, perhaps to recognize a recovery anniversary in the program.

At the end of the meeting, before you run out the door, somebody will ask for your phone number. People in the fellowship know how hard it is for some to make it back to that next meeting; about half don't come back. Newcomers think it won't work for them or that they are not that bad *yet*. They worry they'll be seen by somebody they know. But a lot of them will return years later in worse shape.

When I came to my second meeting, people welcomed me and they knew my name. They reached out to shake my hand. I was on a see-saw of wanting to keep gambling on the one side and wanting to be with these people I was getting to like on the other side. Those people are what kept me there. At meetings, I walked in and people remembered me. They made me feel good, even when I was not able to feel good about myself.

They assigned me a person I could talk to when I needed to talk to somebody—a sort of temporary sponsor.

They suggested I look among the group for a continuing sponsor on my own: somebody I could relate to and who was willing to guide me. I found a guy who had been in the program for three or four years and I was comfortable with him. You don't have to be social with your sponsor, just feel comfortable with phoning him or her in the dark hours when you have a fight with your spouse or have some other crisis and feel the urge to get out and gamble to make yourself feel better.

Sheila tells me that Frank, my early sponsor, literally saved me during the first couple of years in recovery. Frank was like a Damon Runyon character: He was in his fifties and had been a box salesman, stealing and borrowing from everybody he could. I know that if he told me to meet him at seven o'clock, day or night, it didn't matter, I just went— to Flushing or Staten Island or New Jersey, or wherever he was schlepping me to—for program activities. He was well-respected, and wherever he took me, I got acknowledgment.

They made me feel good, even when I was not able to feel good about myself.

The first suggestion I received in the program was to get two more jobs and to put the money into Sheila's hands. They knew I had debts to pay and shouldn't have idle time to gamble or to think about gambling. And they knew I couldn't be walking around with lots of dough in my pocket. Money, free time, and a lack of accountability were ingredients for disaster.

If a gambler has the urge, he needs money in order to play, and in the early stages of recovery the paycheck should be in somebody else's hands. If there is no family to handle his or her money, it should be in control of the sponsor or someone else who understands the intensity of the gambling urge and can be trusted.

When I was gambling and felt hot, if I had six dollars in my pocket that meant two dollars for tolls, two dollars for admission to the track, and two dollars to bet the daily double. You know, money burns a hole in the resolve.

I believe that true recovery means being able to take care of your own life needs and make your own decisions. The twelve-step program's pressure relief meeting begins to address that. It's a difficult problem. The gambler has to live on an allowance and it can't be an endless thing. Genuine personal needs come first. But at some point he must be able to handle his own daily needs like a normal person, and we can't say exactly when to turn it over to him. The sponsor has to be a guiding voice through this and the whole twelve-step process:

The Twelve Steps of Recovery

1. We admitted we were powerless over gambling—that our lives had become unmanageable.

2. Came to believe that a power greater than ourselves could restore us to a normal way of thinking and living.

3. Made a decision to turn our will and our lives over to the care of this Power of our own understanding.

4. Made a searching and fearless moral and financial inventory of ourselves.

5. Admitted to ourselves and to another human being the exact nature of our wrongs.

6. Were entirely ready to have these defects of character removed.

7. Humbly asked God (of our understanding) to remove our shortcomings.

8. Made a list of all persons we had harmed and became willing to make amends to them all.

9. Made direct amends to such people wherever possible, except when to do so would injure them or others.

10. Continued to take personal inventory and when we were wrong, promptly admitted it.

11. Sought through prayer and meditation to improve our conscious contact with God as we understood Him, praying only for knowledge of His will for us and the power to carry that out.

12. Having made an effort to practice these principles in all our affairs, we tried to carry this message to other compulsive gamblers.

Printed with permission of Gamblers Anonymous® International Service Office.

Relapse and Maintaining Recovery

Very few people walk into a twelve-step program and stop from day one. Most of us have relapsed at least once in the beginning. I know when I hear somebody at a meeting tell of being at a racetrack and describing his horse nosing into the lead approaching the finish line, I can feel my juices flowing.

When I ran the Council on Compulsive Gambling in New Jersey, part of my contract called for me to meet with people from the Casino Council Commission and the Racing Association, but in *my* office not theirs. I knew I couldn't meet with people in one room while there was racing on the other side of the door. I knew myself well enough by then.

At one of our twelve-step meetings, there was a woman who, in addition to gambling, was also dealing with a drinking problem. She had to make the decision whether to go to her daughter's wedding. It was a terribly difficult challenge. She was in very early recovery, very shaky. She knew she couldn't stand being around alcohol all day and she wouldn't ask her daughter to have an alcohol-free wedding. So she decided, "I won't go. I will be in church."

That was her respect for how vulnerable she knew she was to her addiction.

Once we took the kids to some fast-food place and the girl behind the counter asked, "Where is Hoover Dam?" I guessed; I didn't know the answer. She said, "Sorry, you didn't win," and rang up our order. If I had won two dollars worth of food my broken brain might have told me, *This is my lucky day*. And I would have headed for the casino.

Life has its unexpected sand traps. I play a little golf, not very well, but enough for a twelve-step member to invite me to play at his club. On the short second hole, there was a sign that promised, "Make a Hole-in-One and Win a Car." I was shaking like a leaf as I addressed the ball. I was afraid to take a swing. I "accidentally" knocked the ball off the tee, so according to the rules of the game now I was shooting for a hole in two—an eagle. I was safe.

For years, people would come up to me on the street and say, "Come on, you're still betting. Who do you like in the football game today?" because they didn't believe I had really stopped. You have to figure out for yourself how to handle that. I stay away from anything that gives me anxiety or messes with my recovery or my serenity. You have to honor yourself.

After all these years of having a sponsor and being one, when Sheila and I go on vacation or on a cruise we make sure there's a meeting in the place we're going or on the ship, and also that I know how to reach people in the program if I need to. I've been to twelve-step meetings in forty-two states and seven countries. At home, a good sponsor will phone almost every day, even to talk for only a few seconds. Maybe I had a fight with my wife or I'm having a bad day and have an urge to gamble, and that call helps. I know how much that daily contact from my sponsor at the beginning made me feel like a big shot; I needed that assurance. And slowly, somewhere along the line, my urge to gamble faded.

I stay away from anything that gives me anxiety or messes with my recovery or my serenity. You have to honor yourself.

In recovery, you begin to work on finding out who you are, and hopefully start spending more time with family instead of thinking about who's going to win the fourth race at Belmont. Over time, the twelve-step process begins to ask for self-evaluation: taking inventory of your assets and liabilities and deciding to make whatever changes are necessary to help you be the person you want to be. That's a lot of punishing work. Even with help from a sponsor and a supportive partner, it could take a long, long time, if it's ever fully completed. The recovery process is about self-awareness and the desire to do better, one day at a time. This was—and is—my inventory:

ARNIE'S DAILY MORAL INVENTORY	
LIABILITIES TO WATCH FOR	ASSETS TO STRIVE FOR
Self-pity	Self-forgetfulness
Self-justification	Accountability
Self-importance	Modesty
Self-condemnation	Self-valuation
Dishonesty	Honesty
Impatience	Patience
Hate	Love
Resentment	Forgiveness
False Pride	Simplicity
Jealousy	Trust
Envy	Generosity
Laziness	Activity
Procrastination	Promptness
Insincerity	Straightforwardness
Negative Thinking	Positive Thinking
Vulgar and Immoral Thinking	High-mindedness

As gamblers get better, they will see positive changes in their lives. Sometimes it's those closest to them who see the changes first. As gamblers get honest with themselves and with others, they begin to see to what extent gambling has ruined lives and strained relationships.

Much of the time in early recovery I was thinking Sheila was going to find some other guy and run away, and then I'd be screwed because everything was now in her name; I had nothing. It was in my head for months that she was going to leave me. Sheila tells me that for the first seven years of our marriage, I had a tic—blinking—and I often had headaches. One time I pulled the phone out of the wall. Those were things I recalled for my inventory.

All that inventory-taking is intended to encourage recovery on a daily basis. That's discussed at every meeting. People go on to discover themselves, then to make amends, confronting things they've done and are not proud of and learning ways to approach or repair the damage, such as working on their marriage. A father may dwell on how he treated his children or his spouse. He may try to be a better friend or coworker. There's a lot of self-examination at this point. You have to face the ways you've hurt yourself and the people you care about with your gambling. You can't make lasting progress without it.

All that inventory-taking is intended to encourage recovery on a daily basis.

The last three steps—Ten, Eleven, and Twelve—are maintenance steps. After you make amends and some real changes in yourself, these three steps tell you to take personal inventory on a daily basis—to stay aware, keep yourself in check, and not let yourself be the ball player who thinks he has the game won before the final whistle. You improve your spiritual life. Then you reach out and help other people. You can become a sponsor, lead a meeting, and do service in the program in some other way. If you can't put your mind into a meaningful state, then you're throwing away what progress you've made. Don't get complacent; that's what fighting relapse is about.

Restitution and Repayment

For the first six months, I was pissed working those extra jobs and giving the money to Sheila, all the while arguing with people in the program who kept saying things I didn't want to hear. I was an arrogant son of a bitch. I had that big ego, even though I had rotten self-esteem. And I didn't believe I was a compulsive gambler; I wasn't even sure what that meant. I still had it in my head that I was going to gamble again down the road. It was just that I didn't have the money to gamble, or that I was having a run of bad luck. I thought I could quit when *I* wanted.

I was running the factory in New Jersey; then I'd go to my second job loading trucks in the Garment Center in Manhattan. On weekends, I was working with a photographer doing weddings and other social events. Frank was dragging me to meetings five or six evenings a week, wherever he decided. At night, I'd get home exhausted and go to sleep. Physically running from place to place wasn't a big deal because while I was gambling for the previous seven years, I would leave the factory, run to the Catskills every night, and get up early to drive to my job. I was always out—always running—so I was used to it.

The only positive thing in my mind at the time was remembering that when I stopped gambling and went to those meetings, Sheila and I had a bank account with $8 in it. That's it—eight bucks in the bank. After I stopped gambling, we were building up money in the account and I felt, eventually, that we were going to buy a house. I was working and we were saving money.

But for years, we were like ships passing in the night. We had almost no communication for at least my first year in the program. Sheila might say the first couple of years. She wasn't even yelling at me anymore; she was fuming on the inside instead. If I never came home, it wouldn't have mattered to either of us. But we weren't fighting; it wasn't like she was begging me to stay. For the most part, we had nothing to fight about.

Still I was refusing to accept that I was a compulsive gambler. From time to time, I'd look in the papers to see how the horses or jockeys I used to bet were doing, and how the pitchers I liked to bet were doing. I still had some intention of going back to gambling because that was something I loved. I was still looking in the newspapers to see what the winning lottery numbers were. God forbid the numbers I used to play came up. I was still thinking I was going to hit a big one, go on a streak, and win a lot of money. I can only imagine how I would have responded to the enormous money offered in today's lotteries. But back then in '68 we didn't have mega-million-dollar lotteries.

I kept bothering Sheila about my earnings that she was harboring, and one day she gave in to frustration. She took fifty dollars from our food envelope and almost threw it at me as if to say, "Go to hell!" I was talking about having two dollars to bet on each race, but then I realized I would bet two dollars on the first race and then in the second race I would bet the other forty-eight. I wouldn't be able to restrain myself. It was like some kind of spiritual awakening.

Before I had committed myself to this so-called twelve-step program, in a meeting they mentioned something called a "pressure relief" group. I certainly knew about pressure. I owed $16,000. Today people come in owing a million or more. In those years, $16,000 for me was three years' salary.

To me, what could "pressure relief" mean but that they were going to give me money? How foolish. What they were talking about was a budget meeting, and I had to bring my wife. They wanted me to put our life into financial order so Sheila and I could live together like human beings: paying our living expenses, paying off our debts—debts I ran up—while still being able to go to the movies and even take a vacation. It was a lofty concept. At least that's what I thought at the time; living responsibly didn't come naturally.

The pressure relief group told us we could do it. For the gambler, this is usually the first time he or she knows how much the electric bill is, how much food costs, or what it costs to get your kid's hair cut because he or she hasn't looked at anything like that, ever. Bills are what other people have to pay. Money is for the bet; bills will take care of themselves . . . later. The gambler has to face this strange new reality and way of thinking. It *doesn't* come naturally.

It was a boost for me when Sheila got involved in the spouse/family aspect of the twelve-step program. It meant something to me that she was trying to understand what I was going through. It was Sheila's role in her program to work with me in identifying and writing down each item of regular expense—things the gambler doesn't pay attention to. There's rent or mortgage, gas and electricity, food money, telephone, kids' clothes and diapers, car insurance, gasoline, and transportation for Sheila. It was no longer just me who had to get around; I had to think about Sheila, too.

If there's alimony to be paid, that comes in here. It's part of recovery that gamblers pay back everyone they owe; all of that comes first. A recovering drug addict doesn't go back and pay off his dealer. A compulsive gambler in recovery pays off his markers though.

The committee at the pressure relief group studied all our paperwork and came back after a couple of weeks with recommendations. We began living life on the new budget. After the family, whatever I had left was for paying back loans from three finance companies, my boss, the bookmaker, and a loan shark; all told I owed thirty-two people money—for both legal and illegal gambling funds.

The program tells gamblers to call all the people they owe and ask for a moratorium; tell them you are in a twelve-step program and you will pay them, but a little at a time. That includes casinos. Banks and credit card people are more difficult because you often can't get through to the people who might make those decisions. At the time I stopped gambling, credit cards were new, and I didn't have one—thank God! Everybody got a tiny piece of me, though, and it took me two-and-a-half years to pay everybody what they were owed.

Even bookmakers and loan sharks will usually give a moratorium—often ninety days. They've heard of twelve-step programs and know there's a chance they'll still get paid by a recovering gambler, even in dribs and drabs. It's still money, and nobody wants to turn down money; anything is better than nothing.

I learned—and I had to learn the hard way—that some gamblers hang on to the myth that they are somehow different: that they're not that bad *yet*. Well, I know better. Sheila knows better, too. And sometimes others you wouldn't suspect also know better. For example, after a few months of paying small sums, I was able to tell my loan shark I was going on vacation and wouldn't be able to pay for two weeks. He said he could accept that. Even *he* didn't try to entice me back. I guess he didn't want to risk that if I started to bet again, he would lose even more money with me.

Nobody believed I could make it at first. But restitution gives hope to the recovering addict. He has tried telling himself that if he doesn't make another bet, things will get better financially because he knows that makes sense logically to most people. Yet in the gamblers' illogical mind, it really doesn't. It's only when he sees in black and white that there can be an end to the debt and hope for financial security, even if it's years down the road, that there's a light at the end of the tunnel.

All those months of putting ten dollars, twenty dollars or thirty dollars in the bank became a point of great pride. We were building a house in Sayreville, New Jersey, about forty-five minutes from my job; once a week I'd go there at lunchtime and watch them building it. Every two-by-four plank I saw them put up would make me think, *Never in my life did I believe I would I have that*. I thought I'd never stop gambling. I thought I would chase a big win and then a bigger win for the rest of my life.

Robert L. Custer, MD, the psychiatrist who was the pioneer in the field of compulsive gambling and treated it on the same level with drug and alcohol addiction, summed it up by pointing out the signs and traits of a gambler in healthy recovery. The compulsive gambler was typically male when Dr. Custer did most of his work. But these signs apply equally to women:

Custer's Signs of Recovery

1. The gambler admits that he has a gambling problem, a sickness, and that his problem isn't his need for money to gamble, win, and recover his debt; and that it is the sickness causing all the troubles and the gambler wants to be rid of it.

2. The gambler begins to gain some understanding of his maladaptive emotional traits, his behaviors, and how they perpetuate his gambling problem.

3. He looks for help in finding a job and resumes work quickly.

4. He soon develops a detailed, long-term budget and institutes a specific plan for restitution of debts owed.

5. He becomes an active member of a twelve-step fellowship and is eager to help others with the same problem.

6. He develops a sincere concern for his family's needs and demonstrates this concern by concrete deeds.

7. He has an increased ability to isolate specific problems, develop a plan to deal with them, and to take necessary action to solve them.

8. There are fewer problems and crises in his life.

9. Decisions he makes are sound ones.

10. He develops a sense of pride in himself, what he is doing, and where he is going.

11. Relationships with his wife, children, and other members of the family improve; he spends more meaningful time with them.

12. He accepts himself more realistically and his strengths and weaknesses, without exaggerating or dwelling on either.

13. As the subject of gambling comes up less frequently, his interest in gambling dwindles.

Adapted from When Luck Runs Out, *by Robert L. Custer, MD, and Harry Milt*

Family Recovery

The family of the gambler suffers, as well. I know Sheila suffered through our marriage for seven long years. She was sick, too, which was why she went to the fellowship for family and friends of compulsive gamblers. In the family fellowship, members learn what makes gamblers tick, why we do it, and why we can't stop. Above all, they learn self-preservation. They learn to help themselves to get better before they try to help the gambler, because they can't help anybody if they can't learn how to live a healthy life of their own. They learn that the gambler may not get better after all, and that they may wind up in prison, a mental health facility, or worse. But they can help themselves to live a better life in spite of those possibilities.

In the family fellowship, members learn what makes gamblers tick, why we do it, and why we can't stop. Above all, they learn self-preservation.

Family members work steps similar to those of compulsive gamblers. I've added a brief explanation following some of these steps.

The Family Twelve-Step Fellowship of Recovery

1. We admitted we were powerless over the gambling problem and that our lives had become unmanageable.

2. Came to believe that a power greater than ourselves could restore us to a normal way of thinking and living.

> *The Gam-Anon Fellowship states that a belief in a higher power along with an honest look at themselves will help to resolve their fears, worries, and suspicions.*

3. Made a decision to turn our will and our lives over to the care of this power of our own understanding.

> *Step Three is the willingness to accept the will of a higher power and to let go of self-will. Self-will is said to be at the very root of bitterness, worries, and unhappiness among members.*

4. Made a searching and fearless moral inventory of ourselves.

> *This can be a very difficult step since most fellowship members have been blaming the gambler for their shortcomings. The fellowship provides a list of personal assets and liabilities to use as a guideline when working on Step Four.*

5. Admitted to ourselves and to another human being the exact nature of our wrongs.

> *A member seeks out a person who can be trusted to share the information from his or her Fourth Step inventory. As the member unloads his or her past, a feeling of freedom and peace of mind enables him or her to continue growing in recovery.*

6. Were entirely ready to have these defects of character removed.

Recognizing and owning personal character defects in Steps Four and Five now allows members to bring about positive change. The fellowship states that many of its members begin working on releasing self-pity and resentment so they can achieve their long-term goal, which is peace of mind.

7. Humbly asked God, of our understanding, to remove our shortcomings.

Having made a decision to turn one's will over to a higher power in Step Three, it is time to humbly ask Him to remove one's shortcomings.

8. Made a list of all persons we had harmed and became willing to make amends to them all.

Members list all those harmed by their own behavior. Early on it can be difficult to realize how one has harmed so many people. Harsh punishment, misdirected anger, and criticizing others can be common reasons for harming family, friends, or coworkers.

9. Made direct amends to such people wherever possible, except when to do so would injure them or others.

Making amends to those harmed is an opportunity to bring about change in the spirit of love, kindness, and general well-being. Step Nine also states that one should be careful not to hurt anyone in the process of making amends.

10. Continued to take personal inventory and when we were wrong promptly admitted it.

> *Complacency can lead back to old feelings and behaviors. Step Ten asks members to reflect on themselves on a daily basis in order to evaluate their own progress or shortcomings. It also requires members to admit to any wrongdoing immediately. Following this step will lead toward spiritual growth and serenity.*

11. Sought through prayer and meditation to improve our conscious contact with God, as we understood Him, praying only for knowledge of His will for us and the power to carry that out.

> *This step will open the door to a new and more spiritual way of living. It is suggested to start each day with a prayer or thought of one's higher power to make each day a better day.*

12. Having made an effort to practice these principles in all our affairs, we tried to carry this message to others.

> *Having had some measure of success in working through the other steps, it is now time to carry out the main purpose of the program, which is to help others in their life who are still suffering from the gambling problem.*

Alternatives to Twelve-Step Programs

Various forms of psychology and psychiatry have been found helpful in battling compulsive gambling, but I haven't found anything more effective than the twelve-step program.

Dr. Custer said he could help a suffering gambler in his office or even by phone, but often he was out. Sometimes he would be out of the country or the call came in the middle of the night when he was sleeping, or he may have just been unavailable. The patient, or person in recovery, needs to know that he can find help around the clock and from end to end on the calendar. When you have those urges, the only diversion is to talk.

With the twelve-step program, not only is a sponsor on call all the time, but the gambler feeling the flash urge to fall back also has a list of phone numbers of other people in his group who can help him through his immediate need. Somebody is always available "right now."

Talk is cheap, but, at the right time, talk is priceless. When I get an urgent call from someone in recovery saying that he feels his resolve weakening, I try to hold him on the phone because I know gambling is an immediate action and focus, so obviously I can't distract him by talking about the afternoon's golf game. Instead, I try to get him to dwell on the memory of how lousy he felt when he was in the depths of his disease and how he made the people he cared for feel. Then I try to get him to recall how good he felt when he was able to resist the urge and how wonderful he felt when he was free from gambling. Ultimately, I have to fall back on telling him not to think about "forever," but to just get through this day or this night.

It may have to be one day at a time. Sometimes we help each other, but sometimes we fail, so you have to really want the help and really seek recovery. Unfortunately, the percentage of people who stick with the twelve-step program until they achieve real recovery is not great because the addiction is so strong.

SHEILA'S EXPERIENCE

I had my own recovery phase, although it wasn't the same kind of recovery as Arnie's. Mine was not recovery from gambling addiction, but from myself and from Arnie. We're still together—stuck with each other through thick and a whole lot of thin, when I was afraid that "until death do us part" meant the eighth race or bookmakers' collection on Monday.

With the understanding I have of myself today, I realize I stuck around because I didn't feel I had any alternative. I was extremely insecure; I had little or no self-esteem. I had no job options, either. I don't think I would have been able to go for a job interview, even if I'd had job options. I was at that point feeling that I was nothing. I must have had a bold thought or two at one point because I researched the cost of being alone. I asked myself, *How much would a rental cost? How much money would I need?* and, *Could I manage on my own with two kids?*

I had my own recovery phase, although it wasn't the same kind of recovery as Arnie's. Mine was not recovery from gambling addiction, but from myself and from Arnie.

But I just couldn't leave Arnie; I was paralyzed; I was stuck. At twenty-five years old, I felt that was the way my life was going to continue. And I wanted to get even—that was my addiction. As Arnie put it, he was married to "that bitch." I would have told anybody who wanted to hear about it just what a terrible person he was. I was careful not to bring up the gambling, so I would do it in different ways. And I got sicker.

One day I asked him what was going on. I said, "Oh, you're in trouble again. Tell me the truth." He said he owed this, owed that. "Okay, we'll sell the stock and we'll pay everything off," I said. I saw by the look on his face that we had no stock—it was gone. And that had been my world; my dream world was based on that stock, and that dream was now gone. How sick I was: I put on my makeup and went to play Mahjong as if nothing had happened.

I went out with a friend one night and she had some issues, too. Her husband was also a compulsive gambler. We sat in some diner until one or two o'clock in the morning, drinking coffee and deliberately stalling from going home. Our goal was to worry our husbands. We wanted to stay out long enough to make our husbands wonder where we were and even call the police.

When I finally drove home to our apartment, Arnie was standing out on the street looking for me. And for me, it was a victorious *Yes! I did it*. I made Arnie worry about me just like I had worried about him and where he was. I wanted payback for all the nights I looked for him.

I relived all the hurt and the fights we had or the times I needed him and he wasn't there for me, especially when he left me in the hospital. I would live off that and replay it in my mind. I thought that if I was angry enough, he wouldn't dare gamble again.

At one point, I noticed he wasn't going to the track, where he usually went on Friday nights with my father. He wasn't saying to me, "Let's go to the track," and I was getting nervous. He'd often drop a bomb on me, saying that he'd been lying to me about some loan he said was paid off. This time I thought, *My God, he isn't gambling; he's going to tell me something big.* I was suspicious . . . something was going to shake loose. I thought he was going to leave me for another woman. What else could it be?

I confronted him during the week: "Tell me the truth. Why are you not going to the racetrack?" He said, "Wait a minute." He went out to the car and came back with a little yellow book from the twelve-step program and threw it on the bed. "Here's where I'm going," he said. "I'm not gambling anymore." He was two weeks into the program.

I was both relieved and frightened. Maybe something was going to get better . . . maybe not. I didn't know what the program was; it just meant that he was going for some kind of help, but what did that mean for me?

Every ounce of anger I had turned inward came out. If he was able to stop gambling then, why did he inflict the pain on me—*me*—for so long? Seven years. It was almost as if it was now safe to treat him with my anger. I was out to hurt him; I was out for revenge. And I thought I had every right to be angry. I had *other* people telling me I had every right to be angry. And this anger inside eventually burned a hole in me.

I was out to hurt him; I was out for revenge.

I needed help. There was a spouse group of the twelve-step fellowship that was all wives and husbands then—now it's for anyone who cares about someone who's trying to deal with the compulsion—and I became a part of it very quickly; it was the first time I felt understood. There were people with husbands like mine, and some of them were doing well. Some husbands had stopped gambling; somebody else had bought a house. For the first time, I had a feeling that life might get better.

The group's philosophy was that what Arnie had was an illness—that nobody does this on purpose. He didn't set out to hurt me; he was in the grasp of something that had so much control over him that he couldn't help himself until he got help elsewhere.

It took a long time for me to change my view. I didn't want to believe what they were telling me. I wanted to believe he did it to hurt me and I wanted him to pay. I belittled him any chance I got. I was nasty and arrogant to him. We weren't together that much at the time, though. That probably was why he didn't reach out to me that much, or maybe he didn't notice. But I know what I was thinking and feeling.

Arnie rarely came home between jobs. If he did have any time, usually he'd go out with his sponsor. We never had dinner together except on Sundays. Whatever anybody in his program wanted him to do, he'd do. Essentially, I had to find a way to live my life and take care of myself, whether Arnie stopped gambling or not.

I began to see changes in Arnie that gave me hope. One time I suggested Arnie take a ride, so he took the kids on the Staten Island Ferry—in the middle of a ball game! Usually he would say, "Are you kidding? Not in middle of a ball game."

I wanted to believe he did it to hurt me
and I wanted him to pay.

He used to give me greeting cards for special occasions. He never signed them. He'd just hand me the birthday card or Mother's Day card and maybe say, "Who else would give you this?" One time after he was in the program for awhile, he gave me a card and signed it, "Love Arnie." And I was showing it off to everyone in my program. It meant so much to me. I was hanging on to those subtle hints for dear life.

Arnie and I had no long-time friends we could count on. We only had friends we gambled with, and now we had gotten rid of them all. We began to socialize only with people in recovery like us. We'd get together at someone's home for coffee, but none of us had any money, so somebody brought coffee and somebody brought milk.

We went to one guy's house in the Brighton Beach section of Brooklyn. We got to a big apartment house, ten stories or more, and realized we didn't know the guy's last name. That's how the twelve-step fellowships work. We *know* each other, we know everything *about* each other, all the gory details, but we don't know each other's last names. Talk about anonymity.

Anyway, to figure out who this guy was, we went looking at the names on the mailboxes and doorbells. We knew he was Italian and the building was full of Jewish people. So we rang all the Italian names and finally got him. We brought a couple of bottles of soda, somebody brought six donuts, and somebody else brought a piece of cake—five or six couples gathered at this guy's house. That was our social life. Everybody there had gambled or was married to a gambler, was broke, and was in early recovery.

One of the biggest changes that came for me was when I started to respect Arnie and then started feeling proud of him. The way he involved himself in helping other people made me proud. I was at a twelve-step conference and a woman I knew came over and said she'd heard me speak, and said,

"If you can't stand him, why not get a divorce? You're always thinking about him; why don't you focus on yourself? You can heal yourself." It was like somebody hit me with a two-by-four. I realized that if I didn't do something, he was going to get the divorce I'd been worrying about because I was no fun to live with. I stopped trying to hurt him. I finally got it that he didn't do this on purpose, he wasn't trying to damage me, and that he was sick.

It's very difficult for addicted gamblers to come to grips with the damage they have done until they see it in black and white. Budgeting has more benefit than just paying debts off; but my fellowship also recommends that a spouse see what part he or she played and if there were things that could have been done differently. The program reminds us that "You are not an innocent bystander."

I saw those fights I had with Arnie differently. He made a choice to run out the door. I could have kept my mouth shut and not acted like such a lunatic. When I would stay up all night long pacing the floor and rubbing my eyes to show him how upset I was, I could have gone to sleep. I had children to take care of.

I finally got it that he didn't do this on purpose, he wasn't trying to damage me, and that he was sick.

He was better now, more like the person I married. I didn't know a non-gambling version of him—he had been doing that since he was a kid. But he was a charmer when I met him, quick to do a favor for somebody, wonderful to his grandmother, and good to his family. He was a nice guy. Over a period of seven years of marriage, he turned into, in my estimation, an animal that would drop his wife on the doorstep of a hospital and not care if she was living or dead.

What I started to see was a nice guy again, a *caring* guy— maybe not for me yet, but at least he was caring for other people now. He was concerned about his children and showed affection to them, and he was back to caring about his mother. That helped. I guess I never stopped loving him, but I was just so angry at what he had done. I started to come to terms with the illness of compulsive gambling and the fact that when Arnie wasn't driven by his addiction, he was a good man. So I made a direct effort to stop trying to beat him up.

It came about from switching focus back to myself and trying to be okay. I was afraid to ever be in that situation again where I felt I couldn't take care of myself and my children. That's when I went back to school part-time. It took a very long time, but I no longer needed revenge.

Maybe I could have gotten myself together earlier, but there was no help for me that I knew of then. All those choices I made, and I finally understood that we were both sick and that I wanted to get well, too. So I listened to suggestions on how to get well and let go of my anger.

The bottom line was that I loved Arnie. I wanted our marriage to work. I had a lot of work to do on myself—to help myself heal from the effects of living with the gambling problem. We had a lot of help along the way, help for ourselves to grow and change, and to heal individually. And we worked hard on our relationship, with the help of the twelve-step fellowship and proper counseling. We are blessed to share this journey together.

A Chart on the Effects of Compulsive Gambling on the Family

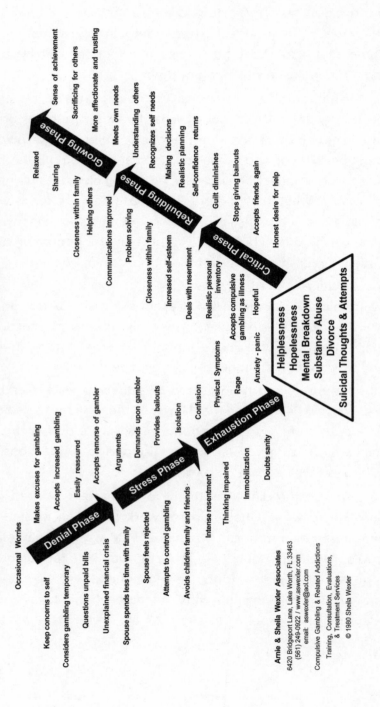

Occasional Worries

Denial Phase

Makes excuses for gambling
Accepts increased gambling
Easily reassured
Accepts remorse of gambler

Keep concerns to self
Considers gambling temporary
Questions unpaid bills
Unexplained financial crisis
Spouse spends less time with family
Spouse feels rejected
Attempts to control gambling
Avoids children family and friends

Stress Phase

Arguments
Demands upon gambler
Provides bailouts
Isolation
Confusion

Intense resentment
Thinking impaired
Immobilization
Doubts sanity

Exhaustion Phase

Physical Symptoms
Rage
Anxiety - panic

Helplessness
Hopelessness
Mental Breakdown
Substance Abuse
Divorce
Suicidal Thoughts & Attempts

Critical Phase

Accepts compulsive gambling as illness
Hopeful
Realistic personal inventory
Deals with resentment
Increased self-esteem
Closeness within family

Stops giving bailouts
Accepts friends again
Honest desire for help

Rebuilding Phase

Guilt diminishes
Self-confidence returns
Realistic planning
Making decisions
Recognizes self needs
Understanding others
Problem solving
Communications improved

Growing Phase

Relaxed
Sharing
Closeness within family
Helping others
Meets own needs
More affectionate and trusting
Sacrificing for others
Sense of achievement

Arnie & Sheila Wexler Associates

6420 Bridgeport Lane, Lake Worth, FL 33463
(561) 249-0922 / www.aswexler.com
email: aswexler@aol.com
Compulsive Gambling & Related Addictions
Training, Consultation, Evaluations,
& Treatment Services
© 1980 Sheila Wexler

NEW LIFE

WHEN WE HAD OUR house built in Sayreville, I was still working at one or another of the many Jonathan Logan subsidiaries and had a number of promotions. I did love that house. But I was still fighting my history of debts and the guilt of what I had done to our marriage with my years of gambling, so the glow of finally owning a home was wearing off. And Sheila was still being chilly to me, which I understand quite well now.

When we moved into our new house, we didn't have $400 to buy a refrigerator. Sears refused credit because we had too much debt. It was painful to be rejected and the pride of having come so far was so great that I sat down in front of the house and cried.

To Sheila, that indicated my remorse and that I was able to reveal genuine emotion. She had been going to the twelve-step recovery group for family members and was open to advice people were giving her, in addition to the things they were saying about me. They were telling her that she needed to focus on herself rather than on me and the financial damage I had inflicted. She went to school to learn court stenography and lasted about a week. She realized that she was going to be no happier at the keyboard. She needed something more and continued searching.

We were in the house two years when she started going to Brookdale Community College, and I had this nervous thought that she was going to find some other guy in school. For three or four years, that thought was stuck in my head. After all, I had wrung out our marriage for six or seven years. Everything we owned was in her name, so I began putting money aside in a vault in case she left. But I got scared when my friend Irving said he went back to gambling after five years in recovery when he started hiding money from his wife. So I brought the money home to Sheila.

I also still had the compulsive gamblers' addiction to lying, which I was good at. It was just one more compulsion; I lied when there was no reason to lie. Looking back, I stayed in recovery because of my ego and because I was a good liar; I wasn't going to admit I had failed. I lied about ridiculous things. If I had Chinese food for lunch, I said I had hot dogs. One time I had a little money in my pocket and I bought a pair of Bally boots for fifty-five dollars. I came home and Sheila asked how much they cost. I said fifteen dollars. A year later she asked again and I told the truth; she caught me in the original lie. What a memory she had for the lies I told. Nothing got by her. For most people, gambling is easier to stop than lying. I suppose that was another landmark of my recovery.

Then I got hit with something I never saw coming that challenged the progress I was making, but also gave me some new ideas.

SHEILA'S EXPERIENCE

It was my dream to live in a house in the suburbs, and now I had my house. It was a beautiful house and I could paint the kitchen the yellow color I had dreamed about. After years of a difficult marriage, it was our home. It was what I thought I always wanted. And yet I was still miserable. I was still unhappy, angry, and *very* resentful. If Arnie had done the right things, we would have had it long ago. I wasn't forgiving him for all that time he disappointed me.

We were still on thin ice. I didn't trust him; I had learned that the hard way. I was still breathing down his neck: his "nagging wife." I should have taken more control of our life together and worked harder to get him away from gambling—but I didn't have enough control of myself to help him. That was what I later learned. It would be another couple of years before I came to terms with myself, with Arnie, and, ultimately, with my life.

Worst of all, when it should have felt like a renewed life for us, he said he didn't feel like he was in love when we got married. It hurt me terribly to hear that, and my mind replayed his words over and over again. I was totally in love when we were married, and now I was thinking, *Am I ever going to love him again?*

In 1972, I started at Brookdale Community College at night—one class. On the campus, there was a Woman's Center that provided the support I needed. When I started school I was very afraid I wouldn't be able to handle it. Through the Woman's Center, I found that there were a number of people in my stage of life who were going back to school. My first class there was English and I loved it. The instructor encouraged me and I got an A. It took five years, but I got my associates degree.

I wanted to do something with gambling treatment based on my experience, but there was no such thing at that time. So, instead, I did an internship at the New Hope Foundation alcohol inpatient treatment center in Marlboro, New Jersey. I stayed on as a volunteer. Two months later I was hired as a counselor in the adult unit, and I was able to introduce a program to treat compulsive gamblers.

At that time, almost nobody was treating compulsive gamblers as addicts. With my experience in the twelve-step programs—both for gamblers and their families—I helped create the New Hope program for gamblers.

It was a one-hundred-bed facility and I was treating adolescents and adults addicted to alcohol and other drugs, eventually moving up the ladder until I was made deputy director in 1989. I liked my hands-on work, and the foundation had regard for my thinking. I'm very proud of that. At that time, almost nobody was treating compulsive gamblers as addicts. With my experience in the twelve-step programs—both for gamblers and their families—I helped create the New Hope program for gamblers. I was teaching other people working at New Hope and helping other rehab programs to treat compulsive gambling.

My education was influenced by Robert L. Custer, MD, who had founded the first recovery center for gamblers and had done a lot of work with the Veterans Administration. He was a real pioneer, who later became influential in Arnie's work. Dr. Custer found that some incoming gambling patients would need a "timeout" before they could become inpatients. Some of our new gambling patients showed symptoms common to cocaine withdrawal. We put those people into a detox center before we began the twenty-eight-day program. The treatment evolved as we went along. We discovered that some of what we thought were cocaine withdrawal symptoms were actually signs of gambling addiction. I was also being influenced by Rena Nora, MD, who was treating gamblers at the Veterans Hospital in New Jersey.

I was thriving in my working life and our relationship at home was moving closer. I saw how much warmth and caring Arnie showed to other people in the twelve-step program and realized that was who he was. He was a thoughtful and loving husband. The man I always hoped he was came shining through. He was a good guy, reaching out and trying to help others through their pain and uncertainty. He knew how difficult it was. The late comedian David Brenner had a line about a new pill to cure compulsive gambling. "What are the odds?" he said. But Arnie knew it was no laughing matter.

Arnie and I were working together on occasion and we would give classes on gambling addiction to various groups and hospitals. By then, we were in a good place in our marriage. He had several promotions at Jonathan Logan, up from the kid sweeping the floor to supervising 500 people in the plant. He was making good money. Then in 1985, United Merchants bought the company and had a meeting telling all the executives their jobs were secure. But six months later they started replacing those people with their own. A year later—

Arnie now says, with mixed emotions—they told him he had done a good job, but they were putting the boss's son in his spot. I'll let Arnie tell that story.

It never dawned on me that I'd get laid off, but it was so much comfort when they told me I'd stay on the payroll until I got a new job—three months, four months. I walked out of the meeting with my anxiety still manageable.

Remember how in *Chitty Chitty Bang Bang* they sang, "From the ashes of disaster grow the roses of success"? That may be true, but it may take some time to flower. And it's hard to think that way when it's happening to you. It was a hard time. I lost my company car. Our son Howie was in his second year at Tufts University. The company paid tuition costs for executives' children, and, with the shake up in the company, that was lost, too.

Sheila became the breadwinner. I said I'd work a flea market if I had to; I knew how to do that. In the '70s, when we were always short of money, I would buy stuff in quantity at markets and closeouts—dolls, radios, shoes, hats, *anything*—and sell them in the parking lot at the factory. She remembers putting it this way: "We were poor before and we didn't love each other. If we're poor now, at least now we have love."

I got a severance package and that would hold us for a while. It was clear: We would do what we had to do. First, we took a home equity loan to keep Howie in college.

When I began the twelve-step program, I moved up the ladder in the fellowship quickly. It was the first time in my life I felt like a big shot—not really a big shot, just that I felt good about myself. I was somebody who others regarded well. As a plant manager I didn't feel special; now I got accolades for working with and helping others. That kept me working in the program, and I became the organization's public relations man for New York.

In the early stages of recovery, I'd struggle through many urges to gamble. I'd see sights on the street and hear things on the radio that would tempt me. The lottery was waving $2 million at me every week. *Boy, I could buy a ticket and get out of trouble.* Kentucky Derby time came and I'd hear things or see them in the newspaper and think, *Wow! It sounds like a lock.* The Mets went on a streak, and I knew baseball: *If they can't lose, I couldn't lose a bet on them.*

The stress on a recovering gambler is often harder to resist in times of crisis. Being cut loose when Jonathan Logan was sold was a crisis. At one stretch, I went to meetings for seventeen days straight. On the seventeenth day, a guy said some stuff to me, and in all that listening and watching something clicked in my mind: *This is crazy.* I realized I was strong enough to continue on my own. I didn't need to hide out in meetings.

The stress on a recovering gambler is often · harder to resist in times of crisis.

In the interim, I was involved in founding the National Council on Compulsive Gambling, based on my experience with my own problem. I had a Rolodex the size of a football that was full of contacts. Through the council, I became friendly with the media and with people in government in order to make them understand problem gambling. Sheila says I worked to a fault as a volunteer, as if it were another compulsion. There was no money involved, but it wasn't my work; it was my passion.

I did a lot of speaking at schools and civic groups. I was seriously campaigning that twenty-four-hour gambling would be a terrible trap for compulsive gamblers in New Jersey when I got a call at home from a top CEO in the gambling business. He asked what I would like to do for the rest of my life and I said, "I'd like to run a helpline for gamblers."

He asked, "How much would that cost?"

I guessed: "$100,000 a year."

He said, "I will get you the money. Just stop talking about twenty-four-hour gambling being bad."

I said I could not do that. And I kept talking about how bad twenty-four hour gambling was.

So we got the helpline started, and I had a roll of stickers made saying, "If you or someone you know has a problem, call 1-800-GAMBLER," and I posted them inside phone booths, toll booths, public bathrooms, on car bumpers, construction sites, wooden fences, etc. I was a man on a mission.

When the interim executive director of the council was asked to resign, I was chairman of the board. Suddenly I had a chance to get bumped up to his job and be the top guy. It had been a non-paying job, but now there was a salary offered—not much, but something, and I wanted that job.

At the same time, Robert Stuckey, MD, was running the Fair Oaks Group of drug and alcohol treatment centers from Summit, New Jersey, and wanted to add gambling addiction to the program. He asked for my help. I'd be paid $100,000 and have a car and an office; it was very attractive. We made a handshake deal with the explanation that I was going to stay in the running for the position with the New Jersey Council, where my heart lay. The council had two more people to interview and they asked the fellow they thought was their best candidate how he would raise money for the organization. He said, "Run a raffle." That's what he said. It wasn't funny. The board didn't laugh.

So I got the job I wanted with the council, and I spoke to any group that would listen. I negotiated with governmental groups and with casinos to deal with problem gamblers—how to recognize them and how to make it known that there was help for people with problems. I had constant calls from all over the country, like the one from the fellow who bet on the Super Bowl coin toss and lost. I listened to phone calls about suicide or just plain panic. Plus, I still had my own compulsion of having to clear my desk every afternoon before I left the office. It wasn't that I *wanted* to have a clean desk; I *had* to have a clean desk or I couldn't leave.

I spoke to any group that would listen. I negotiated with governmental groups and with casinos to deal with problem gamblers—how to recognize them and how to make it known that there was help for people with problems.

One of the things I'm most proud of is that with the help of Chuck Hardwick, then speaker of the New Jersey Assembly, the state legislature was convinced to mandate that all casino advertising include: "If you or someone you know has a gambling problem, call 1-800-GAMBLER." That was the first time any casinos had to put up signs about gambling problems. They were not happy about that to say the least.

In December of 1991, I was conducting a seminar in Atlantic City when I began to have pains in my chest, back, and arms. I went back to my hotel, lay down, and the pains became worse. I was fifty-five years old. The hotel phoned for an ambulance. They wheeled me out of the hotel into the Atlantic City Medical Center, where I spent twenty hours in a bed in a hallway, and the care didn't get much better from there. Sheila is always there for me, so after three days she made a phone call to another doctor who got me to Morristown Medical Center where a balloon angioplasty was prepared.

They tell me that during the procedure, while I was sedated, my heart stopped for twenty seconds. I felt like I had an out-of-body experience during that time, as if I was in the air looking down, not realizing I was in a hospital. There were a lot of people running around and loud voices. I was swinging my arms to move them out of my way. I could see nurses at the monitor that my doctors were using to guide the angiogram. When I came out of sedation, still on the table, I told the nurse, "I'm sorry I hit you." She said, "You didn't." They finished the procedure.

The next day I told Sheila what I remembered. She said the doctor told her that I didn't know what I was talking about. The blockage was cleared. I would be fine. It was a good thing my hospital gown hid the black-and-blue marks on my chest from the pounding that brought me back because I don't think I wanted to see them.

For two months, I couldn't go to work at the council, so Sheila took the calls for me. Every twinge I felt, I thought I was dying. I was scared; she was scared. I thought I'd never be okay. Gradually, I came to realize why I was compelled to clean my desk before I left the council at night, same as when I was at Jonathan Logan: It was because of my own compulsive nature, not because of the boss.

We would be on the beach on a Sunday and my phone would ring. Or it would ring in the middle of the night. I felt compelled to answer, every time. We thought I was going to work myself into another heart attack if I didn't back away from some of the pressure. I had to work shorter hours.

Some years before, we had bought a tiny bungalow a block from the ocean in Bradley Beach for $40,000. We called it our hideaway, primitive as it was. We didn't need the kind of house we felt we needed before. The heart experience made us think about acting on our ambition of working together, before it was too late. I knew how good a partner Sheila was. The New Hope Foundation asked her to stay, but we decided to strike out on our own. We took loans on the Sayreville house to pay tuition for our two kids in college, and we saved all we could so we could move. Then we sold the Sayreville house—our home for eighteen years.

In 1994, we walked away from our jobs and decided we could work together and take our show on the road. We had always daydreamed about living and working in Florida. I told the council I was leaving and they offered me a $20,000 raise, but I turned it down. At a nice going-away dinner, a council member presented me with a roll of those 1-800-GAMBLER stickers like the ones I had made. It was nice to feel appreciated, even though we were leaving. Today's jargon might say we were "reinventing" ourselves.

Sheila had lots of academic and hands-on experience treating addiction, including compulsive gambling. I had years of participating, observing my own recovery, and observing the recovery of others and sometimes their failures, too. Sheila's excellent with communication; she knows how to spell and uses correct grammar. The only thing I know how to do is talk; I remember the living hell of breaking my compulsion, and I'm able to talk about it. We fit together like a jigsaw puzzle.

If our planned partnership didn't work out, she could go back to New Hope, and I would not be ashamed to work the flea markets again.

Sheila and I thought we could turn to a lifestyle of reduced stress for ourselves and, at the same time, reach more people who needed help and education. We could grow as the gambling industry grew. At first, Sheila was excited by the prospect and I wasn't. Then I was excited and Sheila wasn't. For eighteen months, we discussed our ideas with a therapist who gave us suggestions about making a business plan.

We upgraded the beach bungalow—600 square feet— with heat and air conditioning, and rented an apartment in Florida for that first winter. Sheila felt that taking a chance on ourselves was exciting, and even romantic. She felt she had never taken a risk in her life before. Around the time I left the council, an old friend from the *Atlantic City Press*, Dan Hennigan, wrote an article on the new plans Sheila and I had, with a headline that said, "Wexler is Gambling Again." Of course, it was *our* "gamble," but I wouldn't use that term—although there were some risky times when we were driving through some rough towns where we feared for our lives before we reached our destination.

We did have good reputations, credentials, lots of experience, and communication skills for dealing with newspapers, radio, and television. We got publicity, and some controversy—which doesn't hurt. Much of our attention was drawn for the Super Bowl, the single biggest day on the calendar for legal and illegal gambling, and college basketball's Final Four, the climax of a month of games that produces an enormous total gambling pool and a lot of broken hearts.

The media would tell of local twelve-step programs for problem gamblers that planned all-day social events and dinners to support members and their families during the temptation of the big events.

It was a time of great casino growth and a time when casino management needed to train floor personnel and executives to recognize and deal with gamblers in trouble. Some states began to require that training. Problem gamblers are trouble for themselves and trouble for casinos, and many casino workers have their own gambling problems. We say that sometimes the problems are greater *behind* the tables than in front. But just as there are recovering alcoholics who can be working bartenders, there are former addicted gamblers who are valued casino workers.

Problem gamblers are trouble for themselves and trouble for casinos, and many casino workers have their own gambling problems.

I can speak the language of the compulsive gambler. Once I had control of my own recovery, I gave talks to athletes at the University of Kentucky and at a number of other schools, and to NCAA groups that didn't recognize the scope of their problems. We have addressed the problem at high school assemblies. We've gone to towns in the Pennsylvania Football Belt and listened to the citizens in the barbershop talk about betting on the local high school teams.

Our first engagement was a presentation to the Indiana Council of Gambling. We would be there for three days and they were supposed to pay us $3,000. It was a promising beginning. We took two weeks to drive to Indiana, making our trip into a sort of second honeymoon, and working out the kinks of our presentation on how to identify a gambling problem. We thought we did well and we were told we would have the check "tomorrow." "The check is in the mail," the program director told us. It turned out he had his own gambling problem and absconded with the funds. We never got paid.

That frightened Sheila. Shook me up, too! We figured we had enough money to last us two years. At about eighteen months, we figured that if we hadn't made headway, we would pull the plug on our adventure and pursue normal jobs. That was our Plan B. As it turned out, we got some more jobs and more speaking engagements to help spread the word about compulsive gambling, so the second year was good. We trained counselors in Minnesota; Sierra Tucson hired us to do training and had us help set up a program. Then Sierra Tucson closed. When it did, we had $18,000 to our name. We were in trouble.

All our work had been with treatment centers and professional counselors; then we began to work for casinos. I went to a party for my friend Joel Jacobson's retirement from the Casino Control Commission and I sat down at a table alone so I could meet new people.

All of a sudden, the table filled with people who knew me, and Donald Trump sat next to me. At first, his people thought I was the enemy because I was helping gamblers— who are their business—to quit. Trump had told them, "Let's find out what Arnie Wexler is about. People gamble; I know that. I'm concerned about people who have a problem."

A year later they asked us to write a responsible gaming program so they could apply for a license in Detroit.

I declined, but they kept calling me. I never intended to work for a casino company. They call it "gaming," but it's still gambling to me.

Then I had this vision of Willie Sutton, who robbed $2 million from banks because, he said, that's where the money was: Where could I help more gamblers than working for a casino company?

We trained 3,000 casino workers for Trump and we did our speaking circuit. In 2000, they decided they didn't need us any more, but Wally Barr, the head of Park Place Entertainment (later renamed Caesars Entertainment), wanted us. We had helped one of his top executives who had a gambling problem get into recovery and he is doing great today. So, we went all over the country training for them, stopping off at their Nevada properties in Reno, Laughlin, and Las Vegas and training at their properties in Mississippi, Louisiana, and Indiana, too. We spent weeks explaining to staff what compulsive gambling is—the signs and symptoms, and when and how to intervene. As they say: "See something, tell somebody." I credit Wally Barr for this: If Caesars' employees recognized addiction, they would put those people on a banned list from all their casinos. They are the only organization I ever saw do that.

Sheila and I have made a good life for ourselves, working together and traveling together. We help people every day. The best part is doing it together—exploring countries and cities in our downtime, not just sitting and waiting in a hotel room.

Many organizations seek our input. We worked at a US Army conference in Japan and figured we probably wouldn't see Japan again, so we took what we were paid and spent a week in Tokyo. People in Sweden were planning to open a casino in Malmö and we worked eight hours a day for five days there. Then we went traveling to Norway and Denmark. We strolled the splendid, yet unpronounceable, walking street of shops in Copenhagen.

Then we started working with Recovery Road, a private addiction treatment facility being developed in West Palm Beach, Florida. We have a feeling for gamblers and their families that's missing from many treatment programs. There *is* recovery. People *do* come back years later and say thanks.

I have a wonderful life. I don't have to lie in bed anymore and pray, *God let me die so I don't have to wake up in the morning.* My gambling and recovery gave me my whole life. If I didn't suffer and endure that part of my life, I wouldn't have this life in recovery today. That's why I can help people.

Sheila says it just a little differently: "If we can get their attention about the disease, they can change their whole lives."

9 ♣

THE BIG PICTURE

THERE IS STILL STRONG resistance to recognizing gambling as a treatable disease rather than a lifetime curse. Pete Rose has a lifetime ban from baseball for gambling on the game. Of course, Rose has never faced his problem and submitted to treatment. But baseball's commissioners have never proposed the possibility of reinstating him. If Rose got into real recovery for his gambling addiction, that might happen. But he has to want help and do the work. That is my opinion.

Sports columnist Larry Merchant wrote a book in 1973, *National Football Lottery,* on gambling within the National Football League. If sports gambling on football in America went away, betting would turn to soccer or some other sport. On two occasions, the NFL Players Association asked Sheila to treat a player with a known gambling habit, but the player's agent refused. He didn't want the player's identity to leak.

There is still strong resistance to recognizing gambling as a treatable disease rather than a lifetime curse.

There have been other players with gambling threats in their midst. When the NCAA, the governing body of college sports, conducts large meetings, they're held in Las Vegas. Go figure.

I thank Robert L. Custer, MD, for his work that resulted in compulsive gambling becoming classified as a recognized disorder. As mentioned in the Acknowledgments, he established the first inpatient program for the treatment of compulsive gambling in 1970 at a Veterans Administration hospital in Ohio, and he helped organize compulsive gambling treatment program at Johns Hopkins University. It was because of his work that the American Psychiatric Association added compulsive gambling to the *Diagnostic and Statistical Manual of Mental Disorders* (*DSM*) in 1980, which, in turn, led to its listing in the International Classification of Diseases. His 1985 book, *When Luck Runs Out,* written with Harry Milt, rings true to this day. As I've said, Bob Custer was my friend and he is greatly responsible for my recovery and my dedication to helping people with my affliction.

He also helped me through the painful post-partum depression of my recovery. I met Dr. Custer and his wife in the early '70s, and we spent time together at his home in Maryland and ours in New Jersey. He was among the few people at the time to present his evaluation of gambling addiction to the public. He was a helper and a teacher—almost a rabbi or priest to me. He took Sheila and me on the road to do presentations and workshops with him, which started us doing the work we do today.

About seven years into my recovery, I fell into a deep depression and could hardly function. Nobody could help me. I'd drive to work weeping that I had to take out the garbage at home; I'd drop the soap in the shower and cry so hard that I couldn't reach down and pick it up. I would speak with Bob on the phone every day; I'd cry and we'd talk for an hour or more. I'd write to him every day about what I was feeling. He knew that my condition was not uncommon to gamblers in recovery, and he talked me through that period.

He got me moving harder and faster into going out to help others. He understood the mentality of the gambler. When Bob died at age sixty-three, I gave the eulogy. I wept.

The eulogy said:

"Sheila and I have lost a good friend. We spent lots of times over the years with Bob and Lillian in our home and theirs. Sheila and I did many presentations all over the country with Bob. When I was in the midst of a major depression Bob talked to me day and night and helped me get through it.

"He was a very special man in my life and helped me find real recovery.

"He was my first mentor and maybe my first sponsor. Because of Doc Custer's encouragement and guidance, Sheila and I do the work we do today. He has greatly influenced our lives and convinced us to be open about the gambling addiction and our recovery.

"He will forever be remembered by Sheila and me and the thousands of gamblers and family members whose lives he touched over the years and all the addicted gamblers and family members in the years to come."

Rabbi Abraham Twerski of Monsey, New York, a psychiatrist and noted author of psychological and spiritual books, was a founder of the Gateway Hospital, a national treatment program in Pittsburgh for pathological gamblers. In his 80s, he helped me understand that the pull of gambling addiction is such that even profoundly religious Jews could be pulled to the casino on the highest of holy days, when doing any business is strictly prohibited, while hiding his religious cap under a baseball cap.

Rabbi Twerski recently wrote a book in which he related a parable about the Passover story of Moses leading the children of Israel out of bondage in Egypt and into the bondage of compulsive gambling. When the rabbi gets a phone call from a tortured gambling addict, he always sends the addict to Sheila and me.

In 2006, twenty-six years after the American Psychiatric Association classified pathological gambling as a psychiatric disorder in their *DSM*, some professionals still had not gotten the word. That year I was testifying at court in West Palm Beach, Florida, when the judge who was hearing the case regarding gambling asked, "Why don't you just stop if you think it's a problem?"

Stopping and Staying Stopped

We've all seen the poster or greeting card proclaiming,

"Today is the first day of the rest of your life." It's a worthy assurance that the past is only prologue. The addict can recover—if he or she wants to badly enough and works at it hard enough. One day at a time is the only way. And there can be some moments—flashes of light—that show me there is more hard work necessary to make others understand the problem.

In 1995, I learned that my understanding of recovery had not reached far enough or wide enough. Sheila and I were conducting a workshop on compulsive gambling for a group of doctors and psychiatrists in Las Vegas. Our presentation had lasted for about four hours when a psychiatrist demanded, "Why are you calling gambling an addiction or a disease? It's a habit."

That remark came 800 years after the legendary British King Canute is said to have commanded the sea not to rise. When the disobedient rising tide soaked his feet and legs, the wise king commented that there were things not even his great power could control.

The addict can recover—if he or she wants to badly enough and works at it hard enough.
One day at a time is the only way.

Most people can gamble and walk away from the table, just as most people can take a drink and walk away from the bar. But some just can't leave without help.

I've known alcoholics who stopped drinking and got jobs as bartenders. They see a constant reminder of what it was like for them and what it could be like if they went back to the bottle. It is quite *sobering*—no pun intended.

But with gamblers, it's different. Outside of the meeting rooms, they don't see or hear other gamblers describe the misery and pain, or see other gamblers in action; they don't get a constant reminder. The message is not refreshed or renewed, and they can easily sink back into the quicksand.

Those gamblers who stopped, and those who try to *stay* stopped, avoid places where people gamble, unless they are visiting a gambling mecca such as Las Vegas or Atlantic City, or some other gambling hot spot, and can't avoid being around it. It's not smart for a problem gambler to spend time in casinos. Some seem to have tried everything from changing geography, taking up new hobbies, and swearing off the race tracks, bars, casinos, or the corner store that sells lottery tickets. Then they slip and swear they didn't see it coming. I don't judge them, and neither should anyone else.

There are some enlightened people out there who understand what a person in recovery has to do. One time, Sheila and I were training casino workers at the Isle of Capri casino in Iowa. A woman who worked in the cage handling money owed a large gambling debt of her own. She had six children and her husband had left her. Management moved her out of the cage to another building where she was working in purchasing. She got into professional treatment, began a twelve-step program, and did well. She's still in recovery today. She couldn't have made it working every day in the cash cage.

There is no magic remedy for the compulsive gambler. Some people can stop if they get help, whether the problem is drugs or gambling or whatever. They can do it. What exists is only the will to get better, do the hard work, and rely on the priceless support of peers. There *is* recovery. I've been there and it's available to those who need a helping hand.

Casinos and Responsible Gaming

In our workshops to casino workers and executives, Sheila and I present an overview of what compulsive gambling looks like. We try to show them what a responsible gaming program is and help them set up something in their own house. Corporate commitment is not just a load of bull. It's partnership with experts who know the problem and provide training and education. Players should be encouraged to recognize when they are heading toward a problem and made aware that they can be helped to find their way out. Casinos should post hotline information in hotel rooms and elevators and on the markers that gamblers sign to gamble on credit.

The gambling industry calls its business "gaming," as if it were all about fun and games. Badminton is a game.

But many casinos still don't want to talk about it, much less try to do something significant about it. Those addicted gamblers are their customers. The gambling industry calls its business "gaming," as if it were all about fun and games. Badminton is a game. The casino operators remind me of the cigarette company executives who testified that they didn't amp up their product and had studies that showed smoking was not harmful. Then, after all those lawsuits, we got the Surgeon General's warning on the packages.

In our presentations, we discuss problem gamblers, from customers who win to bitter losers, and, in the gambling industry, from chambermaids up to the presidents of the companies who also have the compulsion; so many casino workers are addicted gamblers.

We have now trained more than 40,000 casino workers and management personnel to know that they can't look a customer in the eye and *see* the problem. They must look into a patron's gambling history. I have seen many a gambler turn a $20,000 line of credit limit into a $100,000 line in a couple of months. Computerized gambling doesn't recognize any signs on its own.

Too many gambling establishments don't *want* to see a problem. I'm trying to help one gambler who had a $50,000 line of credit in Atlantic City. He went to four casinos with the same ownership and they gave him $50,000 credit in each casino, and he ended up owing them over $200,000. The next weekend they gave him a trip to Las Vegas and $32,000 more credit. It was only business. The same corporation states they have the best responsible gaming program.

Some people won't leave a slot machine because they think it's lucky or because they think it's due to pay off, or won't leave a table because they're winning. Often management will bring a drink or sandwich to a high roller who refuses to leave a table, even to go to the bathroom. Some of them leave wet seats because they won't leave a lucky table or slot machine. They're called "wetters." That should be a clue that they have a problem.

The problem of gambling is hardly limited to people who play for big money they can afford to lose. One of the worst problems I've seen was a $2 bettor who owed $20,000 and was sleeping in a car for months. The problem gambler could have Michael Jordan's money and that wouldn't diminish the problem; it's about what it does to your life, not about the money you spend. Some people just have deeper pockets. If they have a problem, they'll hit bottom eventually, too.

Twelve-Step Recovery and Anonymity

I believe we make a mistake in hiding our names in twelve-step programs. Although anonymity is encouraged, we have a recognized disease that we have to treat for the rest of our lives, and we shouldn't be ashamed of that. And nowadays there are twelve-step meetings in all fifty states, and goodness knows how many countries, which tells me what the public's needs are.

I believe we make a mistake in hiding our names in twelve-step programs.

We should accept ourselves as diabetics do with their lives of continual blood sugar testing and regular medication. Diabetics are up front to friends and loved ones about their dietary restrictions and what they must do to manage their disease. If we can accept diabetes or any other disease of the body, why not gambling addiction? Why the shame? Why be anonymous about our recovery?

Eventually, the public has to recognize and accept our disease. We need not let our addiction define us, but rather let our recovery define us. We have some wonderful people in recovery doing great things for themselves and for others.

Long-Term Recovery

Let no one who has gone through all of the Twelve Steps call him- or herself a "recovered" gambler. There is no graduation diploma for completion of study. Like education, it's a lifetime process. How you continue your study is up to you. I'm still a student of the game. I'm a "recovering" gambler. I don't miss the sensation of gambling anymore, but I hear some people in recovery say they have never again experienced a high like they got from winning or losing or just placing a bet; I fear for them.

For me, there is no greater high than seeing a person who once begged for help who is now on the road to recovery. I still believe the best way to keep my recovery going is to reach out to other gamblers in trouble. It helps me remember who I am, and how much pain I was in when I came for help. It is the way of the twelve-step fellowship that has essentially saved my life.

Meetings I go to now are not limited to discussions on gambling. I know the people there and they know me. There's nothing hidden and conversation is comfortable. One guy says he must not allow himself to watch a baseball game because of the twelve-step program; he threw away his Red Sox cap because it made him remember too much. He also says he can't watch his son's Little League games, and he can't take his kids to a major league game. But there are no absolute rules in the program. You decide what works for you and how you can live with yourself. I still love baseball, for example, and Sheila and I love to go to the games.

I teach coping skills, such as don't let an argument with the wife and kids, or a business setback, push you back into the escape of gambling. It's not worth it.

Compulsive gambling is like glaucoma; it's treatable. If you have glaucoma and you're supposed to put drops in your eyes every day, you'd be a damned fool not to. If you have a gambling problem, don't place a bet today. And get help.

If I buy an instant lottery ticket with my morning newspaper and win five dollars, I could be in a casino by tonight. With the brain of an addict, you're not able to walk away. You have to be on guard *all* the time—whether a day at a time or an hour at a time.

It's been all these years since my last bet and I'm still on guard.

For the first couple of years, I had to fight off a lot of urges, wanting to go back. Maybe I had a personal relationship breakdown or it was the time I lost my job. Those created big urges. Maybe I didn't know how to cope, but I had the support of my sponsor and the other people in the program. As we go on, we hit bumps in the road. I haven't had a strong urge in a lot of years. But after forty-six years, I cannot watch fifteen seconds of the featured TV race without automatically thinking the inside or outside horse is going to catch the leader. I shun it.

I never gambled in a casino, so seeing a casino doesn't bother me. And I'm not a football fan; I'm a baseball fan and I can watch a game for the enjoyment without thinking of gambling. I do feel anxiety about seeing poker or horse racing, though.

For all the similarities, every gambler is different and needs to recognize what triggers him or her.

Some people say there are certain words that trigger an emotional response. It's common language to say, "I bet it snows tonight," or, "We can parlay" a trip to Los Angeles with one to San Francisco. Censorship is not in my thinking. Some people say, "Don't buy newspapers because the point spreads are listed" or "Throw away your Red Sox cap" because you used to bet baseball. Or that there's danger in going to your son's Little League game.

There are no rules in the twelve-step program, only suggestions. My aim is to go back to a normal way of living; recovering gamblers should be able to safely handle money as they move down the road into real recovery.

I don't look at a game as a betting agent anymore. I would not go to the racetrack just to watch; I went there only to bet, not to look at some horse's ass.

Some people in recovery won't go on a cruise because there's a casino on the ship. I went with twenty-one recovering gamblers and spouses on a cruise that had a casino on Deck 5, so we all walked on Deck 6. What do you do when you go for milk and there's a lottery machine next to the cooler? You can't avoid all those things in this day and age.

A few years ago I got a call from a man who said the pill he took for Parkinson's disease caused him to be a compulsive gambler. I thought, *What bull!* Then I got several calls and e-mails with the same story. I learn something new every day. A recent medical study concluded that Parkinson's patients are about five times more likely to become pathological gamblers. Eventually, that might provide greater understanding of gambling addiction. The *Journal of Gambling Studies* urges that Parkinson's patients be screened for gambling problems. Scientists theorize that the drugs that counter the shortage of dopamine in Parkinson's patients' brains influence the pleasure and reward centers of their brains, perhaps encouraging compulsive behavior such as gambling. More study is needed; perhaps gambling addicts need to be screened for Parkinson's.

I know a fellow who was in recovery and abstinent from gambling for thirty-eight years. Three years ago he went to the NCAA Final Four basketball tournament, which he always wanted to see. He started to bet again and now he can't stop. He owned real estate and he lost three houses and a Cadillac. It can happen; there are no guarantees. Like I said, I had to be on guard all the time, especially in the beginning.

Some people say the recovering gambler should put all assets in the spouse's name in early recovery. If you have no access to money and have an urge, it's hard to gamble.

Handling investments, buying a house, getting married, starting a business—there are many common financial risks associated with day-to-day life. Recovery aims to make it possible for compulsive gamblers to eventually understand which they can safely manage.

I don't own stocks, personally. For me, watching the daily ups and downs of the stock market is too much like being drawn to the day's racing results. In 1990, my aunt wanted to give me $20,000 of stock in a drug company. I turned it down; I thought it wouldn't be good for me to have it. A few months later an envelope came addressed to Sheila. It was the stock certificates. So every day, twenty times a day, I was checking the fluctuations. I was totally obsessed, so Sheila gave the stock to a broker to hold. That went on for six months. I had been in recovery for twenty-two years and still I was getting juiced by the action. When Sheila asked me if I ever looked at the stock prices and I said twenty times a day, she sold it the next day.

If an investment is the mortgage on a house to live in, that is a normal financial transaction; you have to live some place. But you shouldn't be investing in ten houses. In the twelve-step program, whoever is managing the budget prescribed by the pressure relief group should attend to the debts and mortgage payments. *First things first.*

Even well into recovery there are bumps in the road. I talk to my sponsor and with Sheila. We also go to the sponsor together and ask how to handle things. Just because you haven't had an urge to gamble for years doesn't mean you're not going to have one tomorrow, and it could be triggered by standard financial transactions. Again—always be on guard.

I got an e-mail from a lady in Poland who wanted to control an urge that, at times, was overwhelming, so one time she locked herself to a radiator in her house for the night and threw the key out the window for her neighbor to set her free in the morning. She felt she couldn't even permit herself to go to the bathroom. As Nancy Reagan said about drugs, "Just say no." Avoidance works best for me.

For any recovery, you have to want it to work. I want the protection of my twelve-step program on vacation, so I find where there's a meeting available. I went to a meeting in Norway where there wasn't a word of English spoken, but the atmosphere reached me. If there's no gamblers' twelve-step meeting, Alcoholics Anonymous is welcoming to those from other fellowships. We call it a "Bill W. meeting"; the principles are the same whether the problem is gambling or some other type of addiction.

I often think of the woman from Rhode Island who asked for our help by e-mail. She had signed herself onto an exclusion list on Memorial Day and later asked if we could get her off the list. We talked to her and that evening she went to a nearby twelve-step meeting. I told her, "The next time you call, you're going to wish you were where you are now. You're going to be worse."

I have the letter she sent back to us. She said, "You saved my life." She often sends us a thank-you note. She isn't alone anymore.

We get a lot of people thanking us for what we do. We try to reach one compulsive gambler at a time, and also one family member at a time who is struggling with a loved one's gambling addiction.

Whether we help people through Arnie and Sheila Wexler Associates or through the many other organizations with whom we work or associate—be it casinos, gaming control boards, or other government agencies, workshops, treatment centers, etc.—we keep in mind that we can't reach everyone. We do the best we can to be available to counsel, educate, and provide advice to anyone who wants to listen.

If you or someone you know has a gambling problem, call me at 1-888-LAST-BET.

Arnie and Sheila Wexler have provided extensive training on compulsive, problem, and underage gambling to more than 40,000 gaming employees and their management and have written responsible gaming programs for major gaming companies. In addition, they have worked with gaming boards and regulators, presented educational workshops nationally and internationally, and have provided expert witness testimony. Sheila Wexler is also the executive director of the Compulsive Gambling Foundation. In addition to running the toll-free, national helpline 1-888-LAST-BET, Arnie and Sheila are consultants to Recovery Road in Palm Beach Gardens, Florida—a Sunspire Health private residential treatment facility for adults with chemical dependency and problem gambling addictions.

ADDITIONAL RESOURCES

Twelve-Step Support Groups
These are the two organizations that Sheila and I work most closely with:

Gamblers Anonymous
International Service Office
P.O. Box 17173
Los Angeles, CA 90017
626-960-3500 or 626-960-3501
Website: gamblersanonymous.org
E-mail: isomain@gamblersanonymous.org

Gam-Anon (for compulsive gamblers' families and other loved ones)
International Service Office, Inc.
P.O. Box 307
Massapequa Park, NY 11762
718-352-1671
Website: gam-anon.org
E-mail: gamanonoffice@gam-anon.org

Other Recovery Resources

Arnie & Sheila Wexler Associates
6420 Bridgeport Lane
Lake Worth, FL 33463
954-501-5270
1-888-LAST-BET (1-888-527-8238) toll-free,
twenty-four-hour hotline
Website: aswexler.com

National Council on Problem Gambling
730 Eleventh St, NW, Ste. 601
Washington, DC 20001
202-547-9204
202-547-9206 fax
1-800-522-4700 toll-free, twenty-four-hour helpline
E-mail: ncpg@ncpgambling.org

Problem Gambling Center
2680 S. Jones Ave., Ste. 1
Las Vegas, NV 89146
702-363-0290
Website: gamblingproblems.com

Books

This book is one of the best books on compulsive gambling that Sheila and I have found, co-written by our mentor and friend, Robert L. Custer, MD:

When Luck Runs Out: Help for Compulsive Gamblers and Their Families
By Robert L. Custer, MD, and Harry Milt
Published by Warner Books, Inc., 1986

You may also want to consider taking a look at these:

A Way to Quit Gambling for Problem Gamblers
By John Chin
Published by iUniverse, 2000

Behind the 8-Ball: A Recovery Guide for the Families of Gamblers
By Linda Berman, MSW, LCSW, and Mary-Ellen Siegel, MSW, LCSW
Published by iUniverse, 2012

Changing for Good: A Revolutionary Six-Stage Program for Overcoming Bad Habits and Moving Your Life Positively Forward
By James O. Prochaska, PhD, John C. Norcross, PhD, and Carlo C. DiClemente, PhD
Published by William Morrow & Co., 1994

Don't Leave It to Chance: A Guide for Families of Problem Gamblers
By Edward J. Federman, PhD, Charles E. Drebing, PhD, and Christopher Krebs, MA
Published by New Harbinger Publications, Inc., 2000

Losing Your Shirt: Recovery for Compulsive Gamblers and Their Families, 2ⁿᵈ Edition
By Mary Heineman
Published by Hazelden, 2001

Overcoming Compulsive Gambling: A Self-Help Guide Using Cognitive Behavioral Techniques
By Alex Blaszczynski
Published by Constable & Robinson, 2010

Personal Financial Strategies for the Loved Ones of Problem Gamblers (booklet)
Published by National Endowment for Financial Education, 2000

Quit Compulsive Gambling: The Action Plan for Gamblers and Their Families
By Gordon Moody, MBE
Published by HarperCollins, 1990

Sex, Drugs, Gambling, and Chocolate: A Workbook for Overcoming Addictions, 2ⁿᵈ Edition
By A. Thomas Horvath
Published by Impact Publishers, Inc., 1998

The Chase: Career of the Compulsive Gambler
By Henry R. Lesieur
Published by Schenkman Publishing Co., 1984

The Gambler
By Fyodor Mikhailovich Dostoevsky
Published by W. W. Norton & Co., 1981

This Must be Hell: A Look at Pathological Gambling, 3ʳᵈ Edition
By Hale Humphrey-Jones, PhD, LPCMH, NCGC
Published by iUniverse, 2009

When the Chips Are Down: Problem Gambling in America
By Rachel A. Volberg
Published by The New Century Foundation, 2001

When the Stakes Are Too High: A Spouse's Struggle to Live with a Compulsive Gambler
By Loraine Allison
Published by Abbey Press, 1992

Readers who think they or someone they know may have a problem can seek professional help locally through counseling services or can contact their state's council on compulsive gambling for further information. A problem gambler may need to use multiple resources to get help.

A WORD FROM STEVE JACOBSON

A long time ago, as careers go, my first professional journalism editor, Jack Mann, offered a profound lesson in one sentence. He said, "Don't tell me; *show me*." That has become the essence of what I've tried to do as a journalist. The way he put it was also the essence of what a newspaper writer tries to do when space is at a premium.

I tried to instill that lesson into Mathew and Neila, my children, as they wrote assignments in school and later took the concept with them into their professional lives.

I think there's an element of that sentiment in my wife Anita's cooking, too, and her teaching of cooking as an art.

Over my years of writing about sports as a reporter and sports columnist, I applied Jack Mann's advice to interviewing and gathering information. I tried to ask questions that couldn't be evaded and couldn't be dismissed with a safe cliché. Sometimes it worked for me. Sometimes it meant letting the subject tell his or her own story. I would shut up and listen.

Why would you want to interrupt what Casey Stengel had to say? "Most people my age are dead at the present time," he said. And, "Why would you want to *think* old just because you *are* old."

Why wouldn't you want to listen to people who have been there?

Red Holzman advised: "Never get your hair cut by a bald-headed barber; he has no respect for your hair." He also taught me to inquire: "Waiter, is your soup hot today?"

As a journalist and now as a friend, I listen to the insights of Dr. Alan Lans, who was the house psychiatrist for the New York Mets and is a drug and alcohol counselor and who simply tries to help people understand themselves and each other.

I talked with Michael Jordan and Mickey Mantle, Joe Torre and Lawrence Taylor, and Mark Messier; I tried to see what made them tick. I learned to spell Krzyzewski on deadline. I heard Don Zimmer tell of the time he and Brooklyn Dodger teammate Johnny Podres went, after a day game, to Roosevelt Raceway and afterward had to take back roads home because they didn't have twenty cents for the toll on Southern State Parkway.

I saw athletes who were paid $100 million a year file for bankruptcy.

Spending nearly forty-five years at *Newsday*, almost always a very good newspaper and sometimes a great one, was a chance to see and observe, and to ask and listen. Anita would be my first reader on a sensitive story. Neila would groan and giggle at a really good pun and say, "Dad, you didn't." She taught me to respect female athletes and not to bog down in gender comparison. Mathew turned his energy and efforts to protecting our environment and the people who live in it.

Like anyone who is a father or ever had one, I learned from my children probably more than they learned from me. I learned honesty from my mother and father, as my father taught me the deception of the curveball. He told me never to bet against Joe Louis, Notre Dame, or the Yankees.

All of which brought me to Arnold and Sheila Wexler and their experiences in the land of the compulsive gambler. I first met Arnie when he was director of the New Jersey Council on Compulsive Gambling, when he would talk at school or when he would tell me about how people ruined their lives with the addiction. He had the information in the pathways of his mind: Ask him the right question and the insight rolled out of his heart.

Sheila had a different kind of emotional perspective on their life together—and she spells better, too!

I think they kept score by the number of people they helped—without ever actually counting. They showed me what they did and how they felt about it.

They didn't have to tell me; they *showed* me.